C. Pink Vandervoort

Janice Calnan

brings a powerful approach to innovation
and leadership development.

Her guiding principals are based on
the work of three well-known specialists—
Ron Lippitt, who co-founded National Training Lab (NTL),
Kathleen Dannemiller of Whole-Scale™ Change,
and Total Quality guru W. Edwards Deming.

A National Certified Counselor (NCC),
Janice is well-respected for her "Principles of Change"
and her leadership development program.

Through her company Calnan & Associates,
Janice is developing the next generation of
leadership thinking—it is collaborative,
timely and a departure from traditional models.

SHIFT:

Secrets of Positive
Change for Organizations
and Their Leaders

Janice M. Calnan

Resources for personal growth and enhanced performance
www.creativebound.com

Published by Creative Bound Inc.
P.O. Box 424
Carp, ON
Canada K0A 1L0
(613) 831-3641
info@creativebound.com

ISBN 0-921165-74-9
Printed and bound in Canada

Editing by Janet Shorten
Book design by Wendelina O'Keefe
Author photo by Robin Spencer

Printing number 10 9 8 7 6 5 4 3 2 1

National Library of Canada Cataloguing in Publication Data

Calnan, Janice
    Shift : secrets of positive change for organizations and their
leaders

Includes bibliographical references.
ISBN 0-921165-74-9

1. Organizational change—Management. 2. Leadership.
I. Title.

HD58.8C33 2001   658.4'06   C2001-901527-5

Acknowledgments

There are many people who have helped to bring this book to life. I give special thanks to all those who have supported me and believed in me...

- Wendy Robinson who singularly spurred me on to write this book;

- Milan Topolovec, Julie Gordon, Sundar Arora, Wayne Ellis, Judy Matheson and Jean Houston who supported my spiritual path and my business development;

- Gail Baird, my publisher, who wanted this book from the first conversation, and her team at Creative Bound Inc.—Barb, Lindsay, Jill, Janet and Wendy;

- Sylvia Laale who handled the early editorial comments and provided clarity for next steps in the book;

- Kathleen Dannemiller, founder of Dannemiller Tyson and Associates in Ann Arbor, Michigan, who taught me a great deal in the realm of organizational diagnosis, design and change and who has provided valuable insights since that early training;

- clients in the automotive industry in Michigan, some

of whose stories have been told and many whose have
not yet been told;

- Wendy Coles, in the automotive manufacturing industry, who opened a huge door for me and encouraged
  new thinking in the industry;
- the men and women in the high-tech industry, namely
  Gilles Motsion, Claire Toplis, Roy Shepard and
  Dave Yeung's team who completed a major shift in
  thinking by completing our leadership development
  program and then moved on to do advanced work in
  innovation and creativity, and to Jennifer Cross and
  Margaret Cooper who helped the whole thing happen;
- Henry Holland, Tony Legg, Harold Magnussen,
  Russell Mellett, André Pion and Chris Seidl who
  shared stories for others to use;
- Ron and Peggy Lippitt and W. Edwards Deming who
  have left this world and have left it a better place.

My sincere and grateful thanks to all of you and to my
daughters, Colleen and Rebecca, otherwise known as Beck
and Col, who give added purpose to my life.

Janice M. Calnan, Leadership Catalyst

Contents

Letter to the Reader

The work of creating change is simple. Most of us complicate it. This book offers a new approach to change, along with a new approach to quality. It undermines the conventional order that people have come to expect and encourages readers to step into a new way of thinking, which allows them to approach their situation with a larger viewpoint. It includes real situations from my work over the past 14 years with senior managers, executives and engineers in several industries. These include international high-tech firms, the automotive industry, the Canadian aerospace industry, health care in the United States and Canada, the media, family-owned businesses, the U.S. military, church boards and education. While the content in each industry is different, the process of bringing people together to create the changes they want and need is similar.

The pyramid, the hierarchical structure of most large companies, isolates. It keeps people from speaking with those who can make a difference in the work that must be done on a daily basis. In the hierarchy there are unwritten rules that say I can't go to my boss's boss to deal with this,

SHIFT

and yet that is the person who could be most helpful. The reader discovers that the place to begin is neither with the boss's boss nor with the boss, but within himself. The process of change always begins with an ending and then there is a new beginning. The reader discovers a new and deeply personal shift in how she herself views her current reality . . . an ending of her old thinking and a new beginning in her thought processes. The material in this book helps to navigate the time between this ending and the new beginning.

For well over a year now I have been working on innovation and change with a senior team in the high-tech industry. Before we began the work I asked the leader why he had called on me to work with his team. "We are already a highly effective team," he said. "We want greater and different results, and we know that if we continue working the way we do now, we'll get the same results we always have. How can we change," he wanted to know, "when we are already using our wisdom and our technical knowledge in the best ways we know how?" He was wise; he knew something different needed to happen. They were ending their individual search for answers and beginning their collective journey. And for that journey wisdom, not intelligence, was required. The difference would be found in their thinking and in their intention.

For this group the task was unusual. While they were about to change their behavior, they would first address their thoughts. They had to look inward, examine their thoughts about their own expectations and suspend their ideas about how things "should" happen. This is a difficult task for technical leaders, many of whom are engineers. Steeped in the engineering/high-tech culture, they are trained to find the right answers. Their methods, while state of the art for engineers and scientists, are not applicable to the technology of human change.

On the one hand *SHIFT* is a concise reference manual to assist the reader with change. It outlines a series of steps through four major principles of change. On the other hand, it constitutes an action plan. The very act of reading it gives rise to a process of change, one that encourages a quiet mind. Various themes are woven throughout the book. While reading Section IV, you may notice a concept that was first introduced in Section II. The material in Section I, "Transforming the Organization," is designed to help you bridge the gap between quantitative forms of measurement and qualitative forms of measurement. Section I is also about my work and learning with the premier Total Quality guru, Dr. W. Edwards Deming. Interspersed throughout the book are Dr. Deming's **14 Principles of Quality Management**. These are listed in total in Appendix One at the end of the book.

SHIFT

Sections II to V define the principles of change that I created and now use extensively in client coaching and team interventions inside organizations. The **4 Principles of Change**, useful in both your work and your life, include:

- Start fully where you are and tell your truth.
- Acknowledge what's working.
- Ask for what you want and need.
- Step aside and notice the evidence of change in the making.

Reading *SHIFT* chapter by chapter is not essential. If you do read it sequentially, you will benefit from the cumulative effect of the ideas presented. But all the topics are interconnected, so you can start anywhere and build on whatever concepts you find that are useful to you. Reading a few pages daily offers support for change in your leadership thinking. Starting with your "thinking" is significant because your thinking is the basis for all your behavior. If you can think of something, there is a good chance that you can do it. If you can't think of what you want to do, where you want to go or how you want to get there, the task will be difficult to accomplish. When you want to change your behavior, you must first change your thoughts. As you read these chapters, please notice what you are thinking.

Each person finds at a glance some element they need to deal with the challenge they face at that moment in their work or their personal life. The material encourages the reader to discover their own current beliefs and values and to continue to weed out older and less effective thought patterns and beliefs. In the process the reader discovers new ideas about how to handle long-standing problems and difficult current situations. For instance, continuously improving interpersonal relationships in the work environment is essential for handling people. Effective leaders know that work gets done through their people. Truly great and effective leaders are committed to continuous improvement in these areas.

The exercises are presented to get you thinking about yourself, your own style and your own situation. What you do with what you learn about yourself is up to you. The purpose of this book is just to help you become more aware.

In the mid-1990s I took the opportunity to study with a truly brilliant woman in the United States, Dr. Jean Houston. Jean runs Mystery School, a year-long program (one weekend a month) that begins in January and ends in December each year. At that time Jean was traveling about 250,000 air miles per year working with heads of state, whole governments, developed and underdeveloped countries, and international

SHIFT

conferences. She describes her work as "changing the thinking of the globe." In fact it's about saving the planet.

The point I am making is that her work is profound and significant. People come to Mystery School from all over North America to expand right-brain learning and to build new ways of thinking. They then return to their regular work in manufacturing, law, high-tech industries, hospitals, consulting and a variety of other sectors to apply new ways of leading. During my year at Mystery School, I met with Jean and a small number of organizational development consultants each Sunday morning for one and a half hours. We shared rich ideas and practices about how to expand leadership and human potential in the workplaces of the nation.

I believe that everyone is a leader somewhere, sometime and somehow. This book is for you in whatever leadership role you are now playing. The best leaders are, first, fully functioning human beings. A senior engineer recently challenged this. He told me that he leaves his personal self at home or in the car when he enters the workplace. When he finished his explanation I smiled and said gently, "Hold on to your chair, Henry. You're about to discover a whole new concept!" People have one basic personality, even though they may temper it according to whether they are at work or at home. Taught to suppress feelings in the workplace, people often think that they are "being different." However, those who work with them experience one person; the same one who is at home is also at work. Are you prone to think of yourself as a completely different person at home from the one you are at work? If so, you are suppressing a rich and living part of yourself.

SHIFT offers simple steps to help you slow down and notice how you contribute to the work environment. It then helps you to move forward in a more purposeful and effective manner. It is about personal change. All change starts with the individual. Since organizations do not exist without their people, it is also about organizational change. It is about creating meaning in work environments where chaos seems rampant.

In order to work effectively and to keep a positive and forward movement, employees and especially their leaders need to have the courage to tell their truth. This means they need to first discover and then speak about what is going on inside themselves. Talking honestly about positive and negative events that impact their ability to do good work ultimately has an impact on quality. Trust, morale and a sense of power increases. You will see later in this book that the human response is an integral part of Total Quality. As people change, so do their organizations.

SHIFT

Carry this book in your briefcase, in your purse or in your coat pocket! If you have the book in your car you can read a few pages when sitting in a traffic jam. Glance at it when you are having lunch alone or when you're riding on the bus or the subway. Start anywhere! Read a few pages at a time! Share it! As you complete the exercises you'll begin to shift your thinking from old routines to new approaches. Your interpersonal skills will improve. You'll have greater peace of mind. Some of you will find yourselves being more introspective. Others may find themselves taking first steps to abandon old habits that no longer serve them.

Use each chapter as a guide to expand your choices about leadership responses. Before long your peers and those who report directly to you will notice that there is something different about you. Your own manager will comment on your changes.

Open the book. It is time to begin.

Introduction

While quality is everyone's responsibility, it is
the responsibility of top management to ensure
an environment where quality can flourish.

W. Edwards Deming

You may want to read this introduction now or at the end of the book. The choice is yours. However, do read it—it's important. It sets the context for the methods and the process of change presented in the book. The introduction also outlines how I got to the point in my career where I work regularly with the human spirit, especially with managers and senior managers. I do this most frequently in the private sector, although I have also worked on a number of projects in the public sector. Many of my clients are engineers and scientists.

During my 10 years in Michigan I had the good fortune to study directly with Dr. W. Edwards Deming, an American statistician renowned for his work in Total Quality. In 1950, at the age of 50, Dr. Deming began a 30-year journey in Japan, where he was credited with helping to turn around the

SHIFT

Japanese economy. He returned to the United States in 1980 to continue his work in developing quality in American business and industry.

In 1989 I attended his four-day seminar called "Out of the Crisis" at Ford Motor Company in Dearborn, Michigan. This was my introduction to his work and to the concept of Total Quality. Although I didn't know it at the time, attending this seminar was a requirement for anyone who wanted to study directly with Dr. Deming in the Deming Study Group.

During this period General Motors was bringing in Dr. Deming to speak to what they called "The Crowd." I first met Dr. Deming in person at one of these "Crowd" meetings. He was introduced to me by Dr. Wendy Coles, a Canadian from Ottawa, who was the lead consultant for the Organizational Development Practice at General Motors Tech Center in Warren, Michigan.

Dr. Deming was relentless about the pursuit of quality in American industries. At the age of 90 he was working with Ford, General Motors and the Kellogg Foundation in Michigan. Each month, when he came to Michigan to work with these clients, he would set aside an evening to meet with those of us who wanted to learn from him. There were 30 to

50 participants at each meeting who would faithfully show up regardless of the weather. We called this group the Deming Study Group. Among the crowd were quality experts and manufacturing people from the automotive industry across the state. There were also first-, second- and third-tier suppliers to the auto industry, engineers and other technical experts, health-care quality specialists, statisticians, scientists, university professors and a number of independent consultants like myself. I had the unfathomable experience of studying directly with Dr. Deming for the next three years. I was part of the Deming Study Group.

As a renowned specialist in statistical analysis and quantitative measurement, Dr. Deming also valued qualitative measurement. During the latter part of his life he lectured on the importance of people. "You statisticians and MBAs have us measuring everything," he would say. "The most important things can't be measured, namely, how people think and how they feel." He so much believed in the voice of employees that he would often begin his work with a company on the shop floor. By doing this he would discover directly from the front-line employees what was happening in the culture. "Your people know your culture," he would say. "When you ask them directly about what's going on, they'll tell you. So pay attention to what they say!"

SHIFT

Dr. Deming believed in the power of people throughout the system to produce quality. His beliefs are reflected in the **14 Principles of Quality Management** that are outlined in Appendix One at the end of this book. This book is about the first 10 principles, the ones that are more intuitive and more challenging to implement.

During my 10 years in Michigan I also had the good fortune to study directly with Dr. Ron Lippitt, co-founder of National Training Lab (NTL), and Kathleen Dannemiller of Dannemiller Tyson and Associates, the designer of Whole-Scale™ Change. Kathie's work is currently practiced globally. Much of the work that I do today is based on the work of these two great change specialists. They provided me with a solid foundation for organizational change work.

Section I

Transforming the Organization

»Shift is needed

1

Are you measuring the right things?

Our culture focuses on numbers as a primary method of measuring change. For the past 14 years I have been working with senior managers and executives, many of them seasoned engineers in the automotive, aerospace and high-tech industries. These highly skilled professionals have learned through their education and professional career experiences that if they can calibrate (or measure) a change in their project or design then they can trust the outcome. Measurement is everything; or, at least, it's crucial to them. Given the speed at which our businesses and manufacturing sites operate today, the belief about having to measure everything, especially with numbers, slows them down and may limit their ability to make good decisions. Numerical (quantitative) measurements are simply not enough.

I am referring specifically to the work of Dr. Deming, a statistician who for much of his professional life relied on numbers, specifically quantitative measures, to determine success.

SHIFT

In the latter part of his life he realized that more was needed: qualitative data were vitally important to the measurement of change. It is qualitative data that are inherent in people's stories about what is happening in their organization.

When we focus on numbers alone as a means of initiating and managing change, we miss a huge piece of what's required to bring about purposeful, quality-driven improvements. Dr. Deming added three components beyond numerical measurements in what he referred to as Profound Knowledge. He reminded North American businesses and manufacturing organizations that in order to bring about major changes the leaders need to:

- understand how people think (qualitative measurement)
- understand how people learn (qualitative measurement)
- understand the system in which they work (qualitative measurement)
- establish some form of quantitative measurement

Qualitative measurement is not about numbers. It is more of an internal calibration, which might also be known as intuition. Barely tangible, intuition requires that we trust feelings deep inside ourselves. These feelings are often hard to describe, let alone measure. One of my colleagues aptly stated, "We may not be able to describe our feelings but we sure know we are alive when we're feeling." Good leaders have learned to trust their feelings. They use feelings, intuition and life experience when they are making major company decisions and thus become more powerful leaders.

Rewards and punishments from childhood often bring powerful memories and associated feelings in the present moment. To get in touch with this, take a look at your internal measurement system, your feelings. To grasp how feelings linger in the body and in our memory, think back to when you were a child in grade school. Let's say a classmate was rewarded for being the "best" at something—something that you also excelled in. What kind of feelings did you experience about yourself when the other child received the reward and you did not? Was it disappointment, hurt, or perhaps a sense of invalidation? Our memory can be experienced in vivid detail at any given moment when we recall a hurtful childhood experience.

You might also have been happy for your classmate. As you recall the earlier experience in this very moment, you might experience the same feelings, in physical form, that were associated with the memory of that earlier event. Our feelings are like that. In many cases we can experience them as if the event were happening today.

What do our cultural norms for rewards and punishments have to do with the workplace today, you might wonder. Here is the anatomy of how things happen in this realm. We reward children in school for being the best at mathematics, sports, music and so on. In a similar way we reward the best athletes with a gold medal. What does the winner of the silver medal determine this to mean about himself? When someone says, "That man over there is married to a real winner," what do we determine this to mean about his spouse, and about our own spouse, for that matter? When we assign the cultural values of "the best" and "the worst," human beings respond in a physical way. They actually experience the feelings that accompany the words "best" and "worst." Experiencing our feelings in positive and negative ways offers a method of internal measurement. This can also be called *qualitative* measurement.

We have come to value numerical measurements in the workplaces of our country, where we are consistently reminded that "if something can't be measured quantitatively with real numbers, it doesn't count." And yet this statement is just not true. To illustrate how numbers are reinforced and feelings tend to be ignored, here is what one senior manager told me:

There is a problem with salaries in the big company, compared to local start-ups. We create a false sense of value by putting people into quartiles and then we say one is better than the other. We convince ourselves that because we have given the team record salary increases they will stay—but we know that we don't match the local start-ups. We also don't value our people. We measure our attrition based on which quartile they are in (top 25 percent, 50 percent, etc.) but our intuition should tell us that we should be more worried that we can't attract experienced people to our company. People come here and more importantly they stay here or leave, based on how they feel. But we never ask them how they feel. And we know that when they are discouraged they start looking around.

We measure what we can experience with our senses, namely, behavioral performance, the things we can see, touch, hear, taste and smell. In this senior manager's corporation the top 5 percent are rewarded with huge bonuses. By doing this, the executive leadership team has inadvertently created an environment where the other 95 percent are demotivated, disempowered, discouraged and restless. These are feelings. Loyalty, creativity and innovation disappear as people update their resumes and begin to look at "outside" opportunities.

SHIFT

Some things are more important to measure than others. Start asking people in your work environment how they feel and what they need to have happen in order for them to succeed. When employees are overloaded with measurement tasks and when they are not invited to say how they themselves could contribute to improvements, their interest in work and their commitment to the company begin to dwindle. If you are in a leadership position, it's important to pay attention to the other kind of measurement, namely qualitative—how people learn, how they think, and how the system works for and against them as they perform their daily responsibilities. Translated, this means you need to pay attention to the perception of managers, employees and even vice-presidents about your company.

Their perception of the situation is significant. If employees don't like the way you lead, they won't support your goals or your direction. Can you afford to have this happen? I suggest that quantitative measurement provides only part of the information that's needed.

Dr. Deming often talked of things that "can't be measured," referring specifically to thoughts and feelings. Feelings cannot be measured except by the one who is feeling them; behavior, however, *can* be measured. Take Brian, for example—a senior manager in a high-tech firm who is faced with having to let employees go. For at least three days he has been thinking about how to do this without causing undue discomfort for anyone, himself included. "How will the employees respond?" he wonders. Brian's concern is one that many managers share.

Brian's behavior can be measured. Those around him can see, just by looking at his face, that he isn't smiling as much as he usually does. The number of times that he smiles in a day can be measured. The strain in his voice and his short, one-word responses in place of his usual friendly conversational style can actually be measured in numbers. While it is important to be able to measure something, in this case it is equally important to discover how Brian thinks, how he learns and what exactly in the organizational system causes him stress.

We might guess that he is stressed about the exit interviews. But the truth is that we really don't know what is going on inside Brian's mind until we speak with him. We can measure his behaviors quantitatively, but we don't really know what his behaviors mean to him. Qualitative measurements are important because they give us additional, essential information. We know that how people feel at work impacts how they behave at work. When they are upset, distressed or worried, their ability to provide maximum performance is often impaired.

SHIFT

I work with a great number of linear thinkers. As our working relationship begins, many of them tend to dismiss "feelings" as unimportant. I ask them, "Does this mean that when an employee is worried and preoccupied with his wife's illness, with his son's poor behavior at school or with his own career opportunities, his feelings are to be ignored?" We then discuss how the client's perception of his own experience impacts his behavior in his professional management role. While his feeling of anxiety, for example, can't be measured quantitatively by anyone but himself, his performance—what he actually does in behavioral terms—can be measured. The notion that "feelings don't matter" is dangerous because feelings do exist. You can feel such things as rage, irritation, joy, passion and sadness, to name a few. Even if you can't put words to the feelings, other people can see evidence of your feelings in your behavior. They can see rage in your face, an angry flailing fist, or compassion in your arms as you hold a a colleague who has just lost a child. And it is feelings of comfort, excitement, confidence and trust that guide major business discussions and technical purchases. Statistics simply support the decisions.

Quality is never about things. It's about people. It's especially about how people think, how they feel and how they perceive the system in which they work. Think about this! What happens to your feelings if you are discouraged from expressing them? Your feelings and concerns at work are often about people, about your colleagues' behaviors and your leaders' responses. What happens to feelings such as concern, irritation, worry or anger when they are held inside? My observation is that they go underground and pop up some-where else as a quality issue. If you are the leader of a team, ask yourself:

- "What am I measuring at work? Is it qualitative or quantitative?"
- "When do I deal with the concerns of my people, the real qualitative data?"
- "How can I get at the work tasks or personal concerns that could be impacting my team's performance? What measurements would help here?"
- "What should I be measuring in order to make a posi-tive difference for my team?"

All of these questions address quality, and our feelings impact quality. Feelings are our blueprint for behavior. While we can't see them, our body definitely experiences them. Failing to address the employee's situation by not talking about work-related and perhaps even personal issues that concern him can create greater problems. He is forced to contain his real responses as he holds his feelings inside. The risk exists that his feelings will show up in some other way that impacts quality.

SHIFT

Remember, feelings are a form of measurement. Have a look at your personal life and notice the parallels at work. By addressing the following questions, discover how you deal with your feelings and consider a few methods to deal with them differently.

Notice how you feel when admiring a painting, one that you find esthetically beautiful. Use this as a base measurement for comparing how you feel when you are at work. Are there times when you feel at peace with your work and confident in just proceeding with it?

Your baby cries. Are you measuring what is happening inside of you? Do you experience fear, irritation, concern? Does anything similar happen when your boss asks you to do yet one more thing? Before you respond to your boss, take a deep breath and notice what is happening inside you. Once you have defined your feelings, let your boss know you have a concern, for example, and say what it is about.

When your son receives an award or when your daughter hits a home run, how do you respond? Do you experience a similar sense of pride about your work projects?

Do you find yourself sad during a certain month or season when you lost a good friend, one of your parents, or even a pet? Does sadness show up at work during this time? What triggers it? Have you lost trusted colleagues through downsizing, project responsibilities or workplace status? All you have to do is acknowledge your feelings and let them be there. Some feelings have to be there for a long time before they resolve themselves. But if you run away from them and try not to feel them, your feelings of sadness will run with you. They will actually get stronger. Take a break and find a quiet spot to let them be present. Once you feel them they will begin to subside.

What feelings appear when your boss praises your good work to your team? Say "thank you" and allow yourself to experience the positive feelings that you have earned. This will help you do even better work as you proceed.

When your boss consistently rewards others and ignores your contribution, what goes on inside you? Describe the feeling. Notice how your feelings impact your work performance. Spend some time when you get home writing about how you felt. When you write about your experience you get the feelings outside of yourself in a concrete way by putting them on paper. When the feelings are on paper, you can actually get rid of them in a physical way by tearing the paper into small pieces and throwing it in the garbage or burning it. This is a very concrete way to get rid of bad feelings.

Your company is beginning to lay people off. Talk with your colleagues about how they feel and in doing so identify the feelings that you have begun to experience. Talking about your feelings allows you to release the tension and fear associated with this kind of event.

2

What is leadership anyway?

> *Leadership can never stop at words. Leaders*
> *must act, and they do so only in the context*
> *of their beliefs. Without action or principles,*
> *no one can become a leader.*
>
> Max DePree, *Leadership Jazz*

Max DePree is the former president and CEO of Herman Miller Furniture in Zeeland, Michigan. The guiding principles and values that seeded the growth of the parent company are the same ones that are prevalent in the company today. It's common to find that the beliefs, values and norms of companies are the same ones that were present among the founding fathers. They get carried along year after year and become established as part of the "bone-deep" beliefs of the current culture.

The characteristics that we assign to a powerful leader are often traits that have been required in the past. They may no

SHIFT

longer be sufficient to lead in the knowledge-based cultures of today. Fixed on a paradigm of known leadership traits, we continue to revere charisma, visibility, good public speaking, logical thinking, a strong sense of order and the ability to measure almost everything. But maybe we're measuring the wrong things. (See Chapter 1, "Are you measuring the right things?" for more on this.)

Change is the norm. When change is managed with human potential in mind, employees are motivated, trusting, creative, innovative and willing to take greater risks to improve quality. All of these skills are required as companies are driven to respond faster, cheaper, with fewer resources and higher quality—all to satisfy greater customer/client/consumer demands. These demands, of course, slow the search for an improved work environment.

This new dynamic demands a significant paradigm shift on the part of the leader. The role of the leader is to be in touch with the beliefs and values of the workforce and to begin by understanding himself. It is the beliefs and values of employees at all levels that allow for quality service and high levels of productivity. When a leader is really in touch with employees he can begin to mobilize employee enthusiasm and capabilities, and capitalize on the emerging business potential.

To make good and timely decisions, leaders need information from all levels of the organization. In most organizations, executive teams consistently receive information through the chain of command, successively filtered by each layer of management. As a result the leader is unable to hear the direct voice of his employees. A forum is required where employees can speak directly with executives about how senior-level decisions really impact quality. Does your company have a forum for this connection to take place?

When a forum for connection is in place, employees experience a meaningful and useful link with their senior team. The way employees are treated is directly linked to their own perception of being valued in the company. What they focus on expands. If they think they are valued, they work hard to provide value. The reverse is also true.

Let's look at fear for a moment. Whenever there is fear in a workplace, quality is at risk. If you are not sure about how fear sounds in your work environment, notice the following comments. All of these were spoken in a fear-based workplace.

- "I had better not say or do that again."
- "There is no way for me to win in this situation."
- "Here we go with more of the same, just packaged differently."

SHIFT

- "Doing this would be a career-limiting move."
- "My manager doesn't listen to our ideas."

In a highly innovative and trusting environment, these statements would sound different.

- "Things were different last month. Let's try this idea again."
- "No matter what we do, it is going to give us insight about the next steps."
- The company tried this before but the circumstances were different."
- "My boss is generally very supportive. He encourages us to try different things."
- "The result was disappointing but the intention and the effort were great. Let's see what we can achieve in this next phase!"

Collaboration is required, and much more. "What more?" you might ask. Have a look at those around you whom you consider to be highly effective and inspiring. Do they display the emerging leadership skills mentioned below? These skills are gentler yet more powerful in nature than the traditional leadership traits.

Declaration—she declares where she stands. Declaration means that you say what you are going to do and then you do it. It also means you are seen by members of the workplace culture to do what you said you would do. In other words, you make a commitment and stand by your word. This is difficult in today's work environment. For example, when an executive team sets a direction, teams in the company begin to move in that direction. If overnight the executive team changes its mind, the teams change their direction. If this happens repeatedly, the pattern is set. This pattern of constant change is counterproductive to quality. A leader needs to reverse it in order to build trust and respect for senior management and allow employees to complete their direction or at least co-ordinate a new direction. A leader who uses declaration is trusted to stand by her word. She "walks her talk." In this way she builds a culture where productivity, service and quality are maintained.

Silence—she finds moments to be still. Many companies, while they value innovation among their employees, inadvertently create the very work environment they wish to avoid—one where creativity and innovation disappear, where quality and timely delivery of products and services is difficult. Innovation requires new thinking, and innovative thoughts enter our mind when we are quiet. This means that down time or quiet time is essential for new and innovative ideas to emerge. Clients tell me: "Being still is controversial. Our workplaces equate stillness and quiet time with being idle and this is unacceptable to our employer." Good leaders know that they need to encourage quiet innovative time along with a forum to share ideas with others.

Not knowing—she suspends her need to have answers. The leader models what she wants her team to do. For example, she wants them to find creative answers to old and current problems. She must therefore model the kind of creativity and openness she wants her team to exhibit. If she keeps talking, the individuals on the team remain silent. By being silent she creates space for their answers to emerge. "It's okay to not know the next step," she tells her team. She minimizes her tendency to be right and to have right answers. She knows that all answers are valuable. Together, the leader and her team provide abilities for new directions. Innovation continues to grow.

Listening—she listens differently. Because she assumes that she does not know what others mean until they tell her, she doesn't jump to conclusions. She asks herself, "What is this person really saying about himself or herself?" She notices behavior and wonders what is happening in the minds of her team members. She is aware that she only *thinks* she knows what others mean when they speak. She also knows that what she hears when others speak is her own interpretation of what the other person said. Can you assume that you know nothing? You will learn much more than you already think you know.

Intuition—she trusts her own intuition and the intuition of others. She understands the difference between intelligence and wisdom. She knows that intelligence comes from book learning, educational training, diplomas and PhD's. It's also based on the information stored in computers. She also knows that while our culture has valued the intellect for hundreds of years, the deeper wisdom of the individual is becoming more valued. Wisdom is a deep sense of knowing. A wise individual offers answers without having to read about something or talk with an expert about it. It's the wisdom of the unconscious mind that leaves a knot in our belly when we push beyond our comfort zone. All you have to do is ask in your mind for a particular answer and the answer often appears. Pay attention!

Flexibility—she is flexible in her style. While she knows about the company rules and regulations she is comfortable bending them. People are her primary concern. She knows that when people are well respected and genuinely valued, she will have their commitment and she will have their best work. She knows that the concept of one right answer is a thing of the past. There are many ways to reach a goal and she is open to finding them.

SHIFT

Authenticity—her communication is open, authentic, assertive and direct. She says what she means and means what she says. Staying "on purpose" is important to her. As a result she questions the intentions of colleagues and of her boss. She asks for clarification. She notices conflict and creates a forum to allow it to surface. Members of her staff feel safe to be fully authentic with her in the lead.

Learning—she encourages individual responsibility for learning. She has encouraged her staff members to identify their own learning needs. When they are ready to grow they need only ask her in order to receive her support and the resources they need to take the next steps.

These skills result from an environment of trust. They align with the leaders described by Warren Bennis and Burt Nanus in their work with CEOs and other company leaders. Bennis and Nanus outline four strategies that outstanding leaders exhibit: they pay attention through vision; they reach meaning through communication; they achieve trust; and they organize for innovative learning.

EXERCISES

List the leadership skills that are rewarded in your company. Where are they stated? Are they part of the mission statement? Are they found in policy form? How do you know which leadership skills to practice in order to be recognized as a good leader?

How is leadership training/professional development handled in your organization? What do you do that represents less obvious leadership skills?

How do you, the leader, build autonomy and independence? For example, identify a problem that exists among your direct reports and notice how you handle their request for your input. What do they do if you have immediate answers? What do they do if you have no answers? Ask them to take on a new project and notice their level of initiative.

Do you reward "right answers" by nodding, smiling, giving verbal recognition such as "Mm-hmm"? Do you praise them? On a scale of 1 to 10 (10 high), how creative would you assess your team to be? Too many answers on your part will limit their creativity.

SHIFT

Now suspend having answers. Be silent! Notice what happens inside you and among the group.

On a scale of 1 to 10, how creative would you assess yourself to be? List some examples of your own creativity in leading others.

3

It takes real courage to call for help.

Systems cannot see themselves. To bring about a major change you need to use an inside specialist who knows that culture and an external consultant who knows the process of how to make change.

W. Edwards Deming

One of my mentors, Kathleen Dannemiller, would often speak about something similar to this idea of Dr. Deming's. "We see the world as we are," she would say, "not as it is." Some of you may know Kathie's company—Dannemiller, Tyson and Associates in Ann Arbor, Michigan—and her work in Whole-Scale™ Change. In the 1970s and 1980s, she and Ron Lippitt, co-founder of National Training Lab, conducted year-long programs on planned organizational change. They called their program the Planned Change Internship, also known as the PCI. I completed the PCI in the summer of 1987.

SHIFT

When Kathie said "We see the world as we are," she was referring to our limited capacity as human beings to really comprehend the perspective of another. What helps to expand our perspective is our ability to talk with others about how our ideas differ. Without connecting with others we tend to repeat our own thoughts and to assume that what we know is right.

Let's look for a moment at how this closed loop of our thinking works. We see a child in a supermarket with his mother and the child is crying. We create some ideas in our minds about what is happening with the child. For example, we might say to ourselves, "He is being punished for something he did," or "He wants a candy bar and his mother won't buy it for him," or "He has pinched his fingers in the grocery cart." As you imagine this scenario you can probably think of other reasons why the child is crying. The truth is that we don't know. We can only know why the child is crying when we ask the child or the mother.

Nevertheless, human beings have a tendency to create a story in their minds about what they see. Presidents, CEOs, managers, senior managers and the rest of us are no exception. Our interpretation is based on our thoughts, beliefs and feelings, which are projected onto the situation at hand. The projection of "I know what's happening" is instantaneous. As human beings we do this daily. Often we don't really know what is happening. To be objective is to talk with those who are directly involved. Otherwise we deal with a limited perspective and not with what's really at hand.

This concept of "knowing what is really going on" is important for an organization embarking on major organizational change. There is a tendency for those in a leadership role to hear about what is happening from their direct reports and then to assume that they know the situation. In the absence of hearing the real story from those who are directly involved, the leader then makes decisions about what to do. An assumption is made by the leader that the manager is telling the story as it really is. This is only partially true. The manager is describing the situation in his own words and not in the words of his team. This is called filtering, and it cannot be avoided unless the leader and the team members talk directly with each other.

Here is the risk. Without the support and direction of an uninvolved third party, such as a consultant, employees feel they are being driven or influenced by their leader's perspective. As with the observer in the supermarket, the leaders miss the real story. Employees have told me that their leaders really don't want to know what they think. Even more emphatically, they "know" their leaders don't really care. But I have found that this is not the case. In my experience, most company leaders really do care and they want to make a difference. The truth is that the leader, or the boss, gets in the way. One of the ways they do this is outlined in the following story.

Scott's company is managing its own culture change and Scott is at the helm. His intentions are honorable. He wants employees to be involved and autonomous, and to demonstrate high levels of initiative when making necessary changes. He has assigned a trainer and a production manager to initiate a culture shift. Employees, management included, are being asked as part of the assessment period to describe the current reality. They have learned through previous experiences with consultants and with earlier assessments to be cautious about how they describe the work situation. Each one knows the truth, the situation that they remember from the earlier exercises. They also know their own manager has the authority and responsibility to carry the news up the line to the senior managers. "If I say what's really happening around here, my manager won't be happy. It isn't safe to tell the truth," they tell me.

Managing your own culture shift and organizational change has its own set of problems. It blocks the path to new ideas because:

- companies using their own facilitators and internal consultants risk imposing a "company view";

- human beings who are more able to change than any other species are also most resistant to change;
- the politics around who has power, resources and money, and who will be offended, gets in the way;
- internal change agents are not necessarily skilled in the process of managing change.

On the other hand, a company that uses external consultants to coach their executives encourages expanded awareness on the part of all those involved. The use of external specialists minimizes the political influence that is always at play.

In our business culture, asking for help is a sign of weakness. I have spoken at numerous conferences over the past 20 years. When I outline some limiting beliefs and begin the sentence "Asking for help is a sign of . . ." the audience of up to 500 people will invariably call out the last word—"weakness." Asking for help is not a sign of weakness. In fact the opposite is true. It takes courage to know yourself and then to ask for what you want and need.

I recommend to companies, as did Dr. Deming, that when they are planning a major change in the organization, they need to use their internal specialists who know the culture and an external consultant who knows the process of change and knows how to deal with natural human resistance. External consultants who are skilled in process consulting (a technique of observing how things happen, noticing how people work together and, more importantly, how they don't) offer the following perspectives:

- They have seen many organizations in similar positions and can envision several possible outcomes long before those inside the system can.
- They have not developed a sense of discouragement from previous company "failures" and therefore are more willing to try something new. They are open to a multitude of possibilities and solutions.
- They are used to challenging old beliefs. As a result, old behaviors and the accompanying resistance, such as "we have always done it this way," fall away.
- They use strategies that reveal the deeper underlying, yet unspoken, concerns of employees, management included.
- They coalesce the support for change across the organization.
- They help internal change agents expand their understanding of how cultures change.

Let's look at change again for a moment, and the natural resistance that accompanies a request for change. Keep in mind that politics is always about relationships. Key to good relationships is trust and open communication even in the face of opposition. As a facilitator, and as one who focuses on the people side of change, I now believe it is important to use several strategies at one time to bring about small-group and system-wide change. This requires that the leader and the consultant work together to manage meaning for employees at all levels. Relationships then develop. Sometimes existing relationships need to improve.

Coaching individual managers and executives is a useful first step. One-on-one coaching allows a client to push past natural resistance about what he believes the company will allow. It also provides a space for him to develop new ideas and to practice new behaviors. Small-group interactions help to deepen commitment. As managers and employees focus on real work assignments they begin to discover that they want similar things. They often realize they have been working at cross purposes, and at this point their ability to hear each other improves. The gap between them lessens. Beyond this we use large group meetings to bring employees and managers together from across the company. Cross-fertilization of ideas happens. Creativity and innovation expands, as does awareness about the culture and the people in it. The whole-system change process is briefly described here. I refer you to the work of Marvin Weisbord in his book *Productive Workplaces* for more details.

Dr. Deming's quote at the beginning of this chapter suggests that managing a system-wide change requires input from inside and from outside the system. When working with a change specialist from outside the system, internal change agents begin to push past their own limiting beliefs about what can and cannot be done. We all have limiting beliefs. Limiting beliefs begin with self-limiting statements such as "I can't do that because . . ." or "We tried that last year and it didn't work" or "Management refused it before so we had better not stick our necks out now."

With an outside perspective to validate their thinking about change strategies, employees push beyond their own limiting beliefs. Change agents, management and employees from across the organization begin to see their situation through new eyes rather than through the mindset of what has happened in the past. Resistance begins to fall away in favor of "Perhaps we could revisit that need" and "You are right; that was a year ago and a lot has changed since then." Using a specialist in change from outside the system helps managers and employees to expand their thinking about what is possible. As resistance begins to disappear they begin to build a work culture that offers what they really need to succeed.

EXERCISES

Courage is required when you start to make changes in your old habits and patterns. The following questions will help you to shift to new habits and patterns.

Imagine that you have a huge task ahead of you and that you probably need help. What steps do you normally take first? List them!

What were you taught in childhood about needing help? What were you taught about asking for help? Write these down.

What do you need at work from the environment, from your own leader, from your peers and from your team in order to succeed? How do these people know what you need? Do they guess or do you tell them directly?

When you need something in order to succeed in your personal life, how do you get what you need? Write the answers down.

4

"Profound Knowledge" surpasses knowledge management.

The process of leading a cultural change in an organization requires serious thought. Ask yourself, "How will change impact the work and the lives of the people who run our company?" My observation is this: decisions are made at the executive level. Behind these decisions is the desire to provide high-quality service and high-quality products to customers. There is also a desire to keep the shareholders happy by ensuring that financial indicators like Price/Earnings (P/E) ratios or the return on investment (ROI) remain high. But the strongest desire concerns the bottom line. Based on their strong beliefs about the value of keeping shareholders happy, the senior executive team runs the risk of creating the very things they are trying to avoid — poor quality, minimum innovation and a fear-based, risk-avoidant culture. Of course, in such a culture top quality cannot be provided. The situation happens something like this.

- Someone, perhaps the media, decides that the market is growing at a slower rate than predicted.
- A major company spokesperson is interviewed by the media and says that there is "no need for alarm."
- The word "alarm" now triggers public attention and investors take notice.
- To prove to investors that the company is serious about managing expenses, there is a first round of company layoffs.
- Those who leave the company have stories to tell. The media is watching, talking with those laid off and reporting "reasons for concern."
- Investors, still cautious, begin to look elsewhere for investment opportunities.
- Now, with all the attention, the economy is showing signs of a downward shift.
- Layoffs, along with the economic downturn, cause those who are laid off to keep from investing.
- Other investors have become conservative and the economy experiences another downturn.
- People stop buying. In the automotive sector, for example, people stop buying cars.
- Steel and plastics manufacturers that supply the auto industry slow down.
- Layoffs spread and there is talk of a recession.

SHIFT

And on it goes. How to stop the trend? The competitive edge in this kind of market exists at the level of employees throughout the company. Employees know what is wrong, and they know how to improve the situation. Rarely are they asked. With an economic downturn managers and people in general begin to "turtle," to pull into their shells. They won't stick their noses out to see what's really happening.

A major shift in thinking is required. Deming called it Profound Knowledge. There are four primary components to consider when you want to manage a major company change:

Understand how people think. People part with their money based on their level of safety. If they have a full-time job and a regular income they may take greater risks in this area. Similarly, when trust is high in the workplace employees share more openly their creative ideas about where they think change needs to happen and where quality can be improved. What we focus on expands. (See Chapter 7, "You're it! Look inside the box!" for more on this.) When we focus on fear we get more fear. Fear surfaces automatically in a company that is downsizing. Risk, innovation, creativity and quality spiral downwards. Confidence in the leaders drops. When confidence in the leadership team is low, risk and innovation disappear. It's critical for the executive team, and for all leaders for that matter, to be in touch with the mindset of their employees. If you are in a leadership role in a company where a fear-based culture resides, pay attention to what people think. Talk with them directly. Open your door to rumors. Learn to drive out fear.

Understand how people learn. There have been volumes written about creating the learning organization. "How" remains a daunting task. One question to ask is, "How do I know that learning is happening?" If you want answers watch the behavior of employees. Ask yourself repeatedly, "What conditions must be present for people to pursue their interest in learning?" Dr. Deming was not sure how people learned. However, he was adamant about the need for managers to understand this and to create a working environment where learning was valued by employees and especially by their management. "The best way I know how to do this is to ask them," he said, "and if you still don't understand, then ask them again." People learn in several ways. They learn by reading, by observing, by talking with others who know the skill that is required, and by combining these methods. If you are the leader what do you know about how people learn? Perhaps it's time to learn more about learning.

SHIFT

Understand the system in which people work. When a company is structured with a single leader at the top, when communication flows from top to bottom, when change happens layer by layer from top to bottom and when each level, especially the front line, "serves up," then quality, healthy risk, innovation and creativity become impossible. The functioning of the system then becomes counter-productive to quality. The larger the bureaucracy, the greater the risks of disfunction. When change happens in an organization it is essential that the executive team has a full understanding of how change impacts the people and the work that the people are engaged in. I am told that in almost every case, executives are more concerned with making profit and pleasing shareholders than in helping their employees provide the best quality and service possible. If you are the leader, do you really understand the impact of your decisions on the people who operate your company on a day-to-day basis?

Develop expanded methods of measuring the shift in culture. The 1980s brought with them a great social pressure to improve quality. It was then that Dr. Deming returned to the United States after a 30-year period in Japan. His work was impressive and Americans wanted a quick fix. In an effort to get this quick fix in their organizations, production managers across North America leaned toward using something they could directly see, namely, measurement, as an important aspect of monitoring a culture change. However, measurement in the absence of implementing the other three areas of Profound Knowledge is simply not enough. Both quantitative and qualitative forms of measurement are required (see Chapter 1).

Marvin Weisbord in *Productive Workplaces* speaks to the people side of change. "When you focus on cost as a way of improving quality, quality goes down and costs go up. When you focus on your people as a way of improving quality, quality goes up and costs go down."

EXERCISES

Do you need to expand how you manage change? Are you using all four areas of Profound Knowledge?

Have you noticed from your leadership position what kinds of measurement are valued in your organization? Are quantitative *and* qualitative measurements being used? Identify several in each area.

Section II

Start Fully Where You
Are and Tell Your Truth

»Shift is about to happen

5

Courage is required!
If you're scared, you're
right on track.

*You want to bring about change without ever
feeling the pain, without ever having to feel
vulnerable. It just doesn't work that way.*

Peter Block, *The Empowered Manager*

I speak regularly with clients about the need for them, as leaders, to have courage. "To do what?" they ask, and I remind them, "to tell the truth about how things work and especially how they don't work, and to talk about your own level of frustration." This isn't easy to do. They were hired because they have the knowledge, skills and talent needed by their company. At the time they were hired their employer recognized their strengths and had some expectation that they would use their skills autonomously to serve the company.

Ken is a manager. He tells me, "Something gets in the way.

SHIFT

The company hired me because I am a star in my field. I have been here six months and it's hard to do some of the things I was hired to do. The system gets in my way. How can I tell the VP (or any boss) about what's really happening? He doesn't want to know."

As I listen to Ken's story two things are on my mind. First, I wonder why he thinks his boss doesn't want to know about the real situation. I also wonder what exactly it is that gets in the way, that keeps Ken from doing the work he was hired to do. So I ask, "What gets in the way and makes it hard to speak about your frustration?" I know that one of the things at stake in a top-down culture is the tendency to manage one's own image. People fear looking bad in the eyes of their leader. Ken confirms this. "If I tell my manager what's happening, he may think I can't manage." "Have you had this conversation with your boss?" I ask. As you might expect, he tells me, "Not exactly." Without a straightforward conversation with his boss, Ken is likely dealing with a limiting belief of his own.

A limiting belief is any belief that minimizes a person's ability to be authentic with someone else. Limiting beliefs prevent personal and professional growth. There are always good reasons for limiting beliefs. For example, Chris is a manager who is concerned about compromise. "If I say what is really happening here it may jeopardize the release time and I know that clients don't want to wait." Another manager, Michelle, has reminded me that "The truth may jeopardize the work of our whole group. The project may even be canceled." As you read these comments and concerns of other managers you can probably think of a few reasons why it gets difficult to tell the truth about situations in the place where you work. Most folks want to create harmony, not frustration, at work. If you tell the truth about how things are not working well you may risk the loss of something you have grown attached to, perhaps a job, a project, colleagues, a way of doing things and ultimately your reputation. For individuals and whole teams, telling the truth can become difficult. There is often a great deal at stake.

This brings to mind the "troublemaker." Generally the troublemaker is someone who has been in the system long enough to see the result of not speaking up. It's the troublemaker who has the courage to speak the truth, no matter what, because he or she feels that there is nothing to lose. I ask clients to think of the troublemaker as the "truth teller" and to learn to value that person's courage.

As we know, telling the truth is difficult when there is fear of a negative response. In Ken's case, his boss might perceive

SHIFT

Ken to be incompetent. However, since Ken has not talked directly with his boss, there is no real data about what his boss thinks except perhaps through the stories of other people in the department. It is important for Ken to decide for himself what his boss is really like. Then he can reformulate his own beliefs about his boss, and decide how to proceed.

There are ongoing cultural elements that impact the situation. I have been told repeatedly during my years as a specialist in human change that the hierarchy "serves up." This makes the boss look good. When things go wrong there is a tendency in the hierarchy to protect the senior people and to pretend that everything is fine. In other words, we are culturally conditioned to soften the truth by telling only part of the truth. Remember, if we say how things really are there may be a negative consequence and someone might get hurt. Most of us don't want to feel bad or to contribute to the plight of another.

Take Gilles, for example. He is a powerful and compassionate leader. In the following situation he offers a great example of how he told the truth. This was not easy to do.

In the past three months our company has had to tighten its belt considerably, and this after a year of exceptional fruition. The belt-tightening was filtering down week after week, first in the area of recognition, then infrastructure (amount of space allocated, types of furniture), and finally compensation. Throughout, the leadership team of my group felt that it was in damage-control mode, trying to keep things under control, hoping and waiting for things to improve. As a leadership team we tried to reconcile what was happening with our values so that we could present this information to the entire team with integrity. I tried to manage expectations but, as you might expect, expectations were extremely high and the leadership was feeling more and more disempowered. I was trying to understand what all these changes meant to me. I knew I had to focus the team on the future and move us out of the "glass half-empty" mentality.

After attending a staff meeting where we were told that stock options we had been planning to distribute were being pulled back, I knew I had to do something. After many hours of internal debate and summoning up my courage I decided that it was time to reset "ground zero." I have known a few people on the leadership team for many years, but about half had joined the team only six months earlier so I was not sure how individuals and the team would react.

At the next leadership meeting, I informed everyone that we were resetting ground zero, which meant not to expect more stock options and not to expect the current restrictions to be lifted. I explained that I did not want to spend the next four months saying, "maybe," "we'll see," "it's a possibility," "I heard we might," etc. I could not spend the next months hoping for something. I wanted to start fresh from the point we were at and I didn't want to compare ourselves to the past. It was important that we look forward, and if recognition came along, to consider it as an improvement. We would still fight to improve but we would not say "but we received more last year." I got a bunch of blank looks.

I definitely caught them off guard. I answered a few questions for clarification and continued the meeting. About 30 minutes later, we were dealing with other issues but the tone of the meeting was different from previous meetings. It had improved. The leadership team was focused on moving forward and there was a sense of "glass half-full" in the room. I was very happy and started to relax. I now feel that the morale of the leadership team is heading in the right direction and that this will spread further throughout the larger team.

"Serving up," or aligning events and gathering data to ensure that the boss looks good, requires a great deal of energy. The boss is human and prone to error. Nevertheless, many organizations do practice serving the boss in preference to serving the employees. When you realize that this is happening, there is a risk and a major cost to consider.

One manager, Tony, referred to the risk in this way:

I can recall a time when I was trying to become a first-level manager. I realized that my boss's boss did not fully understand the negative impact he was having on the team. I gently shared my opinion with him. Explained how I could be part of the solution. I was promoted that afternoon and we worked together to fix our organization's issues. This would normally be viewed in a large company like ours as a career-limiting move. It took courage to do it.

It's true. Tony had courage. The organizational culture, regardless of the industry, offers daily clues that remind people not to tell the truth as it really is. "Someone will be angry or hurt." "Someone will be put in jeopardy." These statements and similar ones show up in the conversation when a client is preparing to be authentic. Remember that it takes courage to challenge the norm and the traditions of the larger system. It takes courage to tell the truth.

To change a situation you must also change how you think about the situation. Gilles had to change his concerns about buffering the feelings of the senior team. Tony had to relinquish the idea that his boss was flawless and that he himself would be punished. They both reached a point where they no longer cared about the consequences. It was more difficult to withhold the truth than it was to speak about it directly.

Speaking about conflict as it is really happening has a number of benefits for a leader:

- He models positive behaviors, the very ones that he wants his team to emulate.
- It helps to develop honesty, integrity and courage in himself and others.
- It improves trust and it opens doors to create a higher-functioning team.
- The beliefs and values of his team get stronger as do those of the organization.
- After he demonstrates this courage the first time he begins to sleep better.
- Productivity and quality improve. The company saves money.

Summary: In the short term you, the manager, might protect yourself by saying nothing. In the long term there are just no guarantees. If you hold your tongue for fear of being punished, you may still be let go for a variety of other reasons, perhaps because you failed to deal with a situation that you knew about. If you say nothing, those who report to you will have difficulty doing their job. In the long run, the loss of integrity and peace of mind is more troublesome.

Being a good leader in today's economy takes courage, first to discover what's going on inside yourself and then to speak about it. The place to start is always inside yourself.

.

EXERCISES

It takes courage to tell your boss that some things are not working well. Notice how this is dealt with in your company. Do people deny that there are problems? Do employees/management pretend that things are fine even when they are not fine? If you are irritated about how meetings happen, for example, do you ignore it or do you talk with others about it? Do you criticize others and then worry about having done it? Notice what you do about this and write it down. Please remember that these are all human tendencies that help you survive a difficult moment. The best way to ensure a win-win situation is to reframe your thoughts and ask for what you want and need. (See Section IV for more on this.)

SHIFT

It takes courage to tell your boss that some things are not working well. When is the last time you did this? Notice what you would like to say to your boss on this very day. Imagine that if you said what you wanted to say about the current situation, improvements would begin in areas of long-standing disagreements. Identify some of the limiting beliefs that keep you from saying exactly what is happening. Turn these beliefs into beliefs that empower and inspire staff.

6

Stop waiting! Now is the perfect moment.

The only place we can live our life is in the moment.
Tich Naht Hahn, nominee, Nobel Peace Prize

I mentioned in the introduction that Dr. Deming spoke regularly at the General Motors Tech Center in Warren, Michigan. Often as many as a few hundred people would show up at the "Crowd Meetings," many of them young, mid-level managers. Through question and answer Dr. Deming encouraged the entire audience to answer in their minds the question at hand regardless of who asked the question. He would probe with questions such as, "Well, what's happening?" "How are you improving quality?" "How are you using innovation?"

At one point Dr. Deming addressed the entire audience with the question "What challenges do you have with implementing quality processes?" A young manager called out, "I have a great idea to improve quality. However, I can't seem to get it started. I'm waiting for my manager to come on board." Without hesitation the master challenged him. "So you have a great idea about improving quality? You want to make changes and you're waiting for your boss to get on board? Guess what? You're gonna die!" The audience laughed and the young manager sank into his seat.

I am sure that many in the audience knew that those who wait keep on waiting. The message was clear. "Don't wait! Start wherever you are and do it now!" It's true that your boss may come on board. However, it sure doesn't seem to happen while you're waiting for him. You have a thought, a great idea? Start talking with others about it! Invite your VP, the director or your manager to consider it. You can start with a comment such as "I've been monitoring quality production (or the quality of service) in this area for a few months now and I have some thoughts on improvement. I would like to talk with you about this. When can we meet?" A variety of things can happen:

- Your boss, whoever that is, the vice-president, the director or manager, can delay his response long enough to probe and to find out more about what you have in mind.
- He can recommend a time for you to come and meet with him.

- You can recommend a time for you to meet with him at his office (or elsewhere).
- The conversation can sit on hold for a while and then surface for discussion again later.

If he doesn't meet with you, you haven't lost a thing. You actually completed what you started out to do—namely, to bring to his awareness the fact that you are thinking about improvements. The fact that you have mentioned your interest and he has heard your request may need some time to simmer. If your boss says nothing, let a bit of time pass and approach the topic again. Sometimes shift happens in an instant and sometimes it happens over time. In the interim you may expand on the ideas that you want to share with him so that when you actually sit together you have more specific ideas to work with.

Change—namely, a shift in thinking—happens in three basic steps:

- First there is an idea, perhaps several thoughts, about some kind of change that would improve a situation.
- Step two is sharing it with others—communication either by talking about it or writing about it.
- The last step is to move into action and in doing so to make the ideas real and concrete.

SHIFT

Thought, word and action . . . that's the process of change.

Several years ago Lanny White, my business partner at the time, and I were contacted by the CEO of a unionized company. The leader wanted us to find out what was going on among employees at lower levels in their organization and to "fix" the morale problems at the front line. He then wanted us to recommend some strategies to help the leadership team deal with the problems. We knew the problems were deeper than what was being described by the leaders about the front line. For example, the entire senior team knew that there were problems among the front-line staff and yet they made no connection to the idea that these problems might have something to do with the leadership team itself.

We knew how this worked. A few years earlier Lanny and I had been trained by Ron Lippitt and Kathleen Dannemiller in the Planned Change Internship in Ann Arbor, Michigan. We learned that if a client wanted us to fix someone else in the system then "there was corruption in the system." We knew that you can't fix someone else without their consent and that whoever points the finger needs to be part of the solution. There were some discoveries to make about what was really going on in this company.

Generally speaking, there is a right way to begin an intervention; often it's with the CEO and the executive team. While this is not always the case, it is certainly the way it happened with this company. The thinking on the part of the senior people about how to lead and what was needed to correct the current problems was the real source of the problem.

Here is how the intervention happened. We began with the request to fix things at the front line. We told the CEO that we would take a look and see what was happening. We invited the CEO and the entire executive team to meet with us afterwards to hear about our discoveries and to discuss next steps. We were to discover that the problems that existed at the front line were not created at the front line.

Our next step was one that W. Edwards Deming would have used. We asked front-line employees what they were really dealing with. We did this by meeting directly with focus groups of union members to hear their story at first hand. They told us that on a daily basis the vice-president of manufacturing had a tendency to change the directives. This meant that any work that had begun the previous day now had to be changed in some way or discarded. Employees at all levels were doing their best to deal with this stop-and-start mentality. Adding fuel to the fire was an underlying tension about the

SHIFT

fact that union and management negotiations were less than
three months away; the executive team wanted smooth negotiations in the upcoming collective agreement. As a result, the
union membership tended to mistrust management at a time
when good relationships were highly desirable on the part of
management.

We quickly discovered that there was no forum in the work
environment for the vice-president of manufacturing to hear
directly from the front-line workers about how his decisions
really affected their ability to do their work well. Union members were increasingly frustrated with constant change. They
felt senior management wasn't listening to them and in fact this
was true, simply because there was no direct conversation
between the two sides. The senior managers were, however, listening to the managers just below the vice-president level. They
were getting a filtered story, as so often happens in hierarchical
work environments. This disconnect between the union and
senior management often makes negotiations difficult.

In examining the data we found that the front line held back
nothing. Through their stories (qualitative data) they told us
about daily changes made by the vice-president of manufacturing and that they had no way to speak with him directly.
Their supervisor's job was to keep the numbers high and to get

the work out the door, so pressure to perform was consistent. The supervisor was repeatedly told to try harder. He felt his hands were tied. While there were other factors contributing to the problem, the constant changes from above, along with the sense of powerlessness among the front-line workers, constituted the real source of the problem. Direct communication between senior management and union needed to happen.

Fixing the front line was not the answer. The methods of leading that were used by the executive team needed to change. We began the change process with them. Because we had hinted at the real source of problems early in the intervention, the executive team was able to recognize their role in the problem. They needed to be part of the solution.

This group of senior managers was waiting for something to happen at the front line. They had to stop waiting for the change to happen at that level. Qualitative data from the front line was helpful. We went straight to employees and heard them directly rather than using a questionnaire because change begins to happen the moment that people are invited to tell their story. As they talk about their situation in the presence of others whom they believe can make a difference, they begin to recognize that they have the power to make a difference themselves simply by telling the truth about the situation.

SHIFT

In this case various members of the executive team who wanted to run their company well and provide top quality for their clients had created the problems unintentionally. They wanted harmonious relationships between management and union, and in an effort to provide this they had told union members what to do rather than invite them into the process of creating what was needed.

After our discussions with the senior managers, commitment to change was adopted fully by the vice-president of manufacturing. It was welcomed by his entire workforce. While much more happened in this client intervention, the stories were told and the situation changed as soon as members of the executive team stopped waiting for others to do the work.

EXERCISES

Stop waiting. Start where you are.

Think of a time at work where you had a great idea, something that could really have improved quality. What did you actually do with your idea? If you shared it how was your idea received? Was your boss receptive? Recall what happened! What was your perception at that time about what went on?

How else can you see the situation now that you are older and wiser?

What do you want in your personal or professional life at this moment? Thinking about it is the first step. Communicating about it by talking to a colleague or writing it down is the second step. What are you waiting for? What single small step would help you move in that direction? Remember, one tiny step leads to another. Commit to yourself to take some action. Notice your thoughts and any resistance that comes into your mind and take that action anyway.

What needs to happen in your workplace? How are you keeping it from happening? Here are some ways that people get in their own way when it comes to making positive change in their life: they get impatient; they get distracted; they experience self-doubt.

7

You're it! Look inside the box!

As a human being you are very powerful, as a leader even more so. Remember, you can do almost anything so long as you don't begin the sentence with "I can't." Keep in mind that all change begins inside you and it begins with a thought, your thought. You *and only you* have total control over how you think, so pay attention to what you think about. Henry Ford, founder of the Ford Automobile Company, said it well when he alluded to the power of thoughts: "Whether you think you can or whether you think you can't, you're right." You have the power to shift your thinking at the exact moment that a thought occurs. This is a fact that is not generally known. We change our circumstances simply by changing how we think about them. It all starts with how we think.

Working as a specialist in organizational change, I learned to bring the whole system together at one time to bring about change. While I believe this technique is often effective, I also believe that we change the world one by one. Sometimes change takes place through the process of a whole group intervention. But often it's simpler than that.

Here is how it happens. When we are passionate about something we talk with others. In doing so we influence them. Christ, Mohammed, Ghandi, Mother Teresa and countless others made the changes that they did by talking with others. They each had a vision, something they believed in strongly and something they talked about with everyone they met. Their passion and vision altered the world. Each took one step and then another toward their vision. That's all there is.

We can change our own life. The process of change is the same. When we have a problem or concern we generally have some idea about a solution. As I tell my clients, all we need to do is ask for an answer. If we practice being still for a few moments we begin to hear that small voice inside that speaks the answer. Once we have created some quiet time we need only ask ourselves, "What would be an appropriate next step here?" Our best answers are always available right inside our mind. Unfortunately, in our fast-paced society we take little time for silence. Look inside the box—the box of your own mind. Change your mind and change your life. That's how it happens.

SHIFT

Whole teams, using a similar process, become more powerful simply by slowing down. The same first step applies. I often ask questions of teams that are similar to the ones that I ask individuals. I am looking for their belief systems and the norms they use to build their workplace community. These are the things inside the box, the box of their own mind and thinking. When they feel stuck I tell them, "Stop for a moment and take a look at your collective thoughts that are interfering with movement. If you can identify them you can change them and think about the situation differently. Then you can apply a different approach." When they do, quality improves.

Whether you are on your own or part of a team, one thing and only one thing gets in your way. Regardless of your title—middle manager, senior executive or front-line supervisor—the thing that gets in your way is your own thoughts. Any resistance or "internal block" is always our own perception. Our perception is the biggest barrier.

André, a senior manager, had the courage to look inside himself and challenge his own resistance. André wanted to improve the way he was leading his team so he started by contacting one of the human resource specialists and asking her to conduct a 360-degree feedback instrument. This meant that he would receive written feedback from different levels in the organization—namely, from his peers, from his direct reports and from his own manager—about how they perceived his leadership skills. These people were contacted and they completed the feedback forms.

After a few weeks had passed André had the feedback from these folks in hand. He began to make the changes that had been suggested in the written forms. André was proud of himself. "Surely others will see the results of my efforts," he thought, "and acknowledge my good work." Six weeks passed and he received a comment from only one of his peers. Much to his surprise, this fellow told him that his direct reports saw no change at all. Discouraged, André began to talk with his peers. He learned a valuable lesson, that without direct communication on his part with his team, they continued to see the situation as they had always seen it. Open, honest and direct communication was needed.

André decided to initiate discussions directly with his team about the written feedback. He invited all the people who provided feedback in a written form to meet with him. He told them he had some questions and hoped they could provide him with some insight. He needed their help to continue learning and growing. He knew that he needed to get at a different thought process in order to change and he did that by tapping

SHIFT

into how others thought about him. André was looking into the box of his old way of thinking.

During the discussions with his direct reports who had offered feedback, he talked about his genuine desire to improve. He shared with his team the comments from their 360-degree feedback instrument and asked them what each comment might mean. He told them, "My perception is limited about what you really mean in your written comments. We need to talk openly about what you want and how I can serve you." This dialogue closed the loop. His direct reports asked him a number of questions. They knew he was being honest in his responses and authentic in his conversation and they could see that he was making significant efforts to change. André was making progress, and the whole team began to understand more about the situation.

André later initiated similar conversations with his boss and his peers. When they were finished he knew much more about what people really thought and what they wanted of him. If he were to keep in touch with them as he grew and changed, he knew that they would be able to do their job better. As he discovered what they really meant, he was able to build an open, honest relationship with his direct reports and with the leadership team. He had to enter the box of his own thinking in order to do this.

Henry, another senior manager, offered this story about where he found change to begin.

The one and only thing we can really control is ourselves. There have been many occasions where I have blamed someone else for my problem when it was I who needed to change. For example, when I was much younger I wondered why some "less qualified" people were getting promoted when I wasn't even being considered. I thought it was due to the upper management not having a clue about what was going on. It wasn't until my girlfriend at the time, now my wife, suggested to me that the upper management don't go out of their way to pick the second best person when the best person is available. She suggested that I should find out what skills I needed to work on to become the best. Great advice! She saw how great I was and later married me.

Change begins in the moment, even in this moment as you read these words. Deep inside yourself you know what improves the flow of work and what does not. For most of us it takes courage to speak about what is happening in the workplace to a boss who has not been open to hearing the truth. However, there is irritation, frustration and upset that accompany work situations that are not working well. These irritations cause a physical response in the body. Just think of a situation where this was going on for you. Perhaps you didn't sleep well, felt nauseous, started to have headaches, lost your appetite, socialized less and had less interest in intimacy with your mate. All of these are physical symptoms that appear when job-related stress is on the increase. There comes a point when these symptoms create greater anxiety than telling your boss the truth at work.

This is when change happens. In this case it takes more energy to stifle your voice and to keep from doing what is right for you than to say what's on your mind. When you reach this point you can't lose a thing by speaking up. My only caution is this. Make sure that when you speak to your boss the changes you ask for are ones you really want. When we are clear about what we really want, and ask for it, chances are high that we will get it.

EXERCISES

These questions will help you step out of the box of your own thinking.

Remember all change begins with how we think. Noticing our thoughts, the box of our own limitations and creativity, is a good first step. The second step in change is to communicate these thoughts either verbally or in written form. Can you notice what you're thinking at this very moment? It helps to know what is in the box: writing down your thoughts helps you to see the contents of your mind on paper. It helps to make your thoughts more concrete.

The third step is to go into action, so think of something you would like to do, a goal you would like to achieve. Write that down too. Over the next few days find a quiet moment each day and just read over what you have written. In ways that are almost indescribable, the groundwork for these goals begins to materialize. Begin to notice tiny steps toward that goal or direction. As soon as you state a goal or ask for what you want and need, in this case in the workplace, it starts to come about. Keep the process going!

Be still and listen to that small inner voice inside yourself. Perhaps that voice is now saying "What small voice?" What is your inner voice saying right now . . . and right now . . . and right now? Listening to that inner voice is an important step because our most meaningful direction comes from inside ourselves. Just be still and listen. Most great ideas enter our mind when we are still. When your frustration is high enough you will want to go into action.

SHIFT

Tap into the box of your own thinking. Identify the conflicts! Do you decide to do something and then decide not? How do you keep change from happening? Which thoughts are blocking your creative ideas? What are the thoughts that keep you from moving ahead? Examples might be "I'm not that good as a manager" or "I can't go after that promotion because I have never done that work before." These are "limiting thoughts." If they stay as they are they will keep you from moving forward.

Once you identify your limiting thoughts you can work with them to turn them around and make them positive. Using the examples above, the first might now be "There are a few great programs that I can take to be a better manager and I'm going to do it" or "I am starting right where I am and applying for that promotion. If I get it I will grow into it. If not then I will know exactly what I have to do to get the next promotion."

Remember to think of conflict as a gift or an opportunity. If you are experiencing conflict with others at work, talk with people whom you think contribute to the conflict. Be curious. Ask why they did or said certain things. Suspend your judgment. Break through their resistance and your own by inviting them to tell their story.

8

What's really
important here?

When I live my life in alignment with my purpose, my life
works. When my life works I know I am operating from my
core beliefs. This is my measurement for being "on purpose."
Purpose is simply stated. It answers the questions:

- What am I here to do?
- Where am I to do it?
- Who am I here to do this with?
- What value do I provide?

I frequently talk with clients about their purpose. As I have
mentioned, many of them are engineers in leadership roles
who describe themselves as linear thinkers. "Why are you
here?" I ask them. I am referring to their overall purpose as a
human being. I pay close attention to their answer. After a
pause they usually say something about their purpose. When
what they say matches what they do in their life's work, I
begin to feel a deep sense of "alignment." My body resonates

SHIFT

with what they say. When a client is "on purpose" with their life's mission and they are living their life according to their core values, I feel a rush of adrenalin. My intuition is at work. I know that their words are in alignment with their beliefs and values. I also know that there is very little work for me to do with them. Much of their work around purpose and direction is already completed. If this has not yet taken place, we focus on how they can align their purpose with their life's work. For most of us this takes some work.

Our passion and commitment and the ability to change ourselves flow effortlessly when we are clear about our life's purpose. When we are living our life "on purpose," our goals are easy to achieve and our life just works. Purpose generally weaves through all aspects of our personal and professional life. There are times when I wonder, as perhaps you do, "How can I manage to do all that I want to do?" and "Are my choices really possible?" I get so caught up in doing, doing, doing, that I grow weary. And then I remember something special. I remember that I have chosen my work and that all my work is aligned with my purpose and with the work of my spirit. When I stay on purpose my life seems effortless. What is the work you have chosen to keep you on purpose in life?

My own purpose is to be clear-thinking, loving, centered and purposeful so that I can assist and influence others, especially those in leadership roles. In attending to my life's purpose I help others attend to their life's purpose. To stay on purpose throughout my life I have chosen several roles unique to me. For example, earlier in my life I was a wife, a nurse and a psychotherapist. Now I am a specialist in change, a coach to executives, a friend, a teacher, and I continue to be a mother. Someday I hope to be a grandmother. I chose these careers to fulfill my life's purpose, although during my earlier years I was unaware of this larger picture.

If, as you read this chapter, you find yourself wondering about your own purpose, just stop for a moment and be silent. (See Chapter 2 for more on the ability to be silent.) Then ask yourself the question, "What is my purpose?" That's all that's needed. Just ask for what you want to know and then pay attention to the thoughts that immediately come to mind. (See Chapter 19 for more on stillness.) The answer may show up in funny ways. For example, a tune may start running through your head. When you recall the words to the tune you realize that these words describe your purpose. Or you might be talking with a colleague or friend on the phone and she starts to talk about her purpose. You realize immediately that what she is describing is also your purpose. When you get off the phone

SHIFT

you decide to write it down. Until you heard her describe her purpose you may have had no idea that she was talking about your purpose as well.

EXERCISES

Sit still with a pen in your hand and ask yourself any one of the following questions, each of which address your purpose in life:

- Why am I here?
- What am I here to do?
- What exactly is my purpose?
- Who am I here to serve?
- What are the unique gifts that I offer?

Take a deep breath, close your eyes and notice any sensations in your body. Write these sensations down on a piece of paper. Now notice the thoughts that come to mind as you experience these sensations. Write these thoughts down. You don't have to understand them, just write them down. At a later date, per- haps in a week when you have forgotten some of what you wrote, take a look at the words again. You may now see them with "new ideas and wisdom." There may be clues in them that help you define your purpose with greater clarity.

Section III

Acknowledge What's Working

»Shift is happening

9

We always have choices.

I tell my client, "We always have choices." In other words, we always have choice about how we perceive things. I am sure that he thinks about the situations he has found himself in and questions my sanity. We talk about his choices in life and he discovers that although all the choices might be difficult, he still has a choice about where to start and how to perceive each situation. Somewhere inside himself he knows where to begin. My job is to help him find that place.

We have a tremendous amount of power as human beings. This is especially true if we are in a management or leadership role or a member of a leadership team. But not everyone in a formal position of authority believes they have power. In the early 1990s I was consulting with a senior team in the automotive supply industry. While this was a union–management situation these circumstances could have happened in any industry or any organization.

SHIFT

I was contacted by the CEO in an automobile hauling company because he was concerned about apathy throughout the plant. "They sound powerless to me," he said, "and I think we need to do something about it. I simply don't know where to begin." The drivers were highly skilled in their jobs. They knew about road safety and about loading and unloading new automobiles on the huge tractor-trailer rigs that we see on the highways. They knew the best routes through cities to the dealerships, and how to minimize damage from low-lying branches to the automobiles they carried. They knew their jobs well.

I started by interviewing the CEO. He told me that the drivers were frustrated and discouraged, so while I suspected that the leaders were also frustrated and discouraged, I went directly to the drivers. I was struck by the drivers' perception about the situation. "Many things are making it difficult for us to do our job," they told me. They saw themselves as being controlled by the system in which they worked and they had good reason to think this way. I listened to their story long enough to realize that they believed they could not make a difference. While there were real problems in how things happened in the plant, the major problem was in their thinking. They saw themselves as being without choice and as such felt powerless.

"Well, who can make a difference here? Who has the power to change things?" I asked. One of them told me that their supervisor could probably make a difference and gave me his number. I went to the supervisor and repeated what I had heard. "Who has the power to make a difference here? The drivers say that you have the power to do something." A similar story emerged. "We just follow orders around here, Janice. We really don't have the power to do much, but the manager might be helpful. Why don't you talk with my manager?"

Well, you may have guessed by now that the story was similar with the manager, who pointed to the director, who in turn pointed to the vice-president and so on, until I found myself back in the CEO's office. "Here is what's happening," I told the CEO. "It seems that everyone is controlled by someone else in the system. Each layer of employee is impacted by the layer immediately above it. No one is willing to challenge the layer above."

Perhaps you can guess what happened next. As I spoke with the senior executive in the company, the CEO, I began to hear the same story that I had heard at every level. "Janice, I can't just change the policies around here. This is a unionized shop. Things take time and some things can't be changed." Then he

SHIFT

added, "And besides, I have a board of directors to think about . . . and the shareholders." The story was the same throughout the entire system. No one had power to make a difference and everyone wanted things to change. "Where could they begin?" I asked myself.

I sat in silence for a while just noticing what was going on. Each layer saw itself as powerless in the larger system. "How could it be," I asked myself, "that an entire system of over three hundred people is powerless?" Each felt that they were not able to do the jobs that they were hired to do. This was even true of the CEO.

The secret was in their thinking. As long as each layer saw itself as being controlled by the layer above or dependent on someone else's decisions, they were incapable of deciding on their own. This is common in a top-down structure. They were powerless because of their beliefs. When an individual, a team or an entire division believes that they have no power, in fact they have no power.

I asked myself, "How might this change?" The answer was immediate. Change happens with the individual and it happens in an instant. As soon as a person sees himself as powerful, he is powerful. The shift needs to happen inside the individual. When we take responsibility for the decisions we make, no matter what the consequence, we are said to be "at cause." Personal and professional power increase.

There is a way out of the dilemma. If you're the one that defined the problem situation, then you must be part of creating the solution. As author and consultant Peter Block says, "If you want to bring about change without ever feeling the pain, without ever having to feel vulnerable . . . it just doesn't work that way." To bring about change it's important to go through the very thing that you are trying to avoid. Face the fear and feel the pain. The truth will set you free. Freedom, joy and fun follow.

The result with this company was profound. It began with the willingness of the CEO to address his own resistance to change. Once he recognized that his own sense of powerlessness was linked to his beliefs, he was able to change his beliefs and make different choices about how to deal with the board, the shareholders, his vice-presidents and managers, etc. A whole-system change process followed, where union and management were able to work together to create a culture of power rather than one of fear and immobilization.

SHIFT

EXERCISES

Remember a time when you believed you had no choice . . . a failing marriage, the breakup of a business partnership, a child on drugs, some kind of conflict in your life. Past or present doesn't matter. Choose one situation. List all your choices even if they were all lousy and seemed impossible at the time. Notice that the situation did change and that you actually had choices. If every choice is bad, you still have a choice about where to begin. There is nothing more to do. Just notice that you have choices.

Sometimes the choice we make is to make no choice. "No choice" is a choice. There is a risk when choosing to make no choice. Someone else steps in and makes the choice for us. I recall the amalgamation of two city newspapers and even the merging of two hospital boards that faced something like this. The senior executives in the hospitals were told to find ways to merge. Conflict ensued and never stopped. Eventually the CEO made the decisions for the executives. No one was happy. Stop right now and notice if there are areas in your personal or professional life where you are not making decisions. What are the risks if this pattern continues? Remember that you have choices even if all are difficult.

10

The best practices are close at hand. Quality is the outcome.

You want to improve quality in your organization?
You are going to find out about the best practices
in other companies and then do the same thing?
You haven't asked your people?
It serves you right.

W. Edwards Deming, The Deming Study Group

Dr. Deming left out the consequences and went straight to the outcome. He was often heard to say ". . . serves you right." He was making an important point. When you search for answers to problems or needs in your own organization by examining best practices in an organization other than your own, you ignore the expertise and knowledge in your own company. You also run the risk of insulting your employees, management included. When your staff feels slighted you have a bigger problem. You began by wanting better ideas and

SHIFT

work practices. Now you may have added resistance on the part of your workforce because you failed to ask for their ideas in the first place.

In the auto industry, for example, quality begins with ideas. Quality includes elaborating on these ideas, creating early designs, building a model, conducting customer focus groups, testing the product, marketing, sales and so on. Ultimately it involves the ability of one group to communicate with another about these ideas. In doing so improvements are continuously created.

With the quality improvement era of the 1980s came the benchmarking trend. This meant that standards for quality were set and awards were given. One company looked at another for ideas about improving quality. This trend has continued until today. But companies can look within for their own ideas for improvement. As company leaders and employees discuss the pros and cons of the work process they also discuss what's possible to improve. If they can imagine improvements they can also implement them. Using your own company experts at the front end of the project is key to success. Communication and vision support the process. Ultimately what works in one company is dependent on that company's product, customer needs, employee skills, and the resources and technology available to provide the product.

You probably know by now that a leader doesn't have all the answers, nor does she need to have them. She does, however, need to know how to find answers. One way to do this is for her to ask her colleagues and her team, "What's working?" and "What do we need to do in order to improve quality?" She asks these questions in order to engage them in the process of change. Both the leader and the team already know what works. They know which direction would be best and they often know their first steps toward their vision. But no one knows better than those who do the job about how to improve quality and to deliver products in timely ways.

So what goes awry? In an earlier chapter I mentioned that people are hired for their knowledge, experience and expertise. This is true for front-line employees and senior executives and all those in between. Together—and I emphasize together— the people in the organization have what's needed to move their company forward. However, it's most often the executive team that assumes the role of defining the direction. I encourage executive clients to adopt a joint approach where all levels of employees and management are working together. It helps to ensure greater commitment throughout the organization for the company mission and vision.

SHIFT

Dr. Deming used to say, "Quality is not the car that rolls off the assembly line, the one that is ultimately bought by the customer. That car is the end result of a total quality process. Quality is required at every step." The process of creating quality begins long before the car reaches the assembly line. It begins with a concept, an idea about what is possible.

The end result of the quality process is the delivery of the car to the customer. Without the employees, managers, suppliers to the industry, and the customers' input throughout the entire quality process, there is no car to sell. It is the wisdom, intelligence, common sense and skill of a multitude of professionals and highly skilled craftsmen that ultimately make the various components and assemble the car. All of these people are part of the automotive business. Quality is the entire process.

When you really want to improve quality in your company, leave the competition alone. Use your own human talent. Use it wisely! Ask your people what they need in order to do the best job for the company! Best practices are close at hand. Build your product and service to be the best by using the ideas and passion of your own people. They know better than anyone else what is needed. They know what it is possible to create.

André is a senior manager in the high-tech industry. He has

completed the program on leadership development and transformational thinking offered by our company, Calnan &
Associates. His peers, his direct reports and his boss are also
involved in this program. They have learned new ways to
think about change and they have learned to apply new leadership behaviors in the context of their real work. This means
that they begin by outlining their situation as it really is. That
isn't always easy to do because not everyone wants to hear the
truth. They then acknowledge what's working, and they ask
for what they want and need in order to do a great job. Finally
they pay attention to even small changes on a daily basis.
They know that it's the small changes that constitute the real
evidence of success.

André's boss is Roy, also a participant in our leadership development program. As the leader, Roy is experiencing heavy
pressure from the senior executive team to get the next release
of their product to market by June 15. It's now March 20.
There are multiple glitches in the system that take more time
than was expected to correct.

André knows what's causing the lag time and asks himself,
"Should I tell Roy about these glitches or not?" If André mentions the lag time he knows that Roy will be annoyed. "I have
watched him do this before," says André. "Roy is single

focused and doesn't like to hear about glitches." André reminds himself that if he is told about the problems, Roy will probably push harder and that this technique just won't help. They need to find a completely different approach.

While he knows that he may have resistance from Roy, André is tired of his own silence. Until now the norm has been to say nothing, but André is now willing to deal with the truth. He is concerned that pressing forward without resolving these glitches will put the entire project at risk. He decides to wait for the next "whole-team meeting" with Roy and then act.

Here is what he did.

Roy opened the meeting by asking the team, "Well, how are things going?" No one said a word. Each knew exactly what André knew. Roy noticed the silence; in fact, he had learned in our leadership development program to notice not only the silence but also what was not being said.

André mustered his courage. "Roy, this project isn't going well. If we continue the way we are going, the entire project will be at risk. We have to make some major changes."

Nobody spoke, Roy included. The silence was heavy. Then

two members of the team spoke up almost in unison. "André is right. Push as we might, we can't get this release out in time." More silence. Tension in the room was heavy. They could hear Roy breathing. They could hear their own heartbeats and feel it in their throats. Several seconds passed.

Finally Roy spoke. All he said was, "Okay, what do we need to do?"

The entire team heaved a sigh of relief. Then they talked about what needed to happen. Over the next several business days the project changed significantly. A component of the design was scrapped. Egos were bruised. However, a better product emerged in time to meet their target date.

The message? "Tell the truth. Stop copying others. Use all your talent. Challenge the status quo and do what works." While this is a good example of the need to tell the truth, the point I am making is this. "Have courage. Challenge the norms. Stop copying others and create an opportunity to use wisely and completely the talent in the company. There comes a point where there is nothing to lose and everything to gain." André was willing. How about you?

SHIFT

Take some time to notice the conversations about best practices in your organization. What are the trends? Do you go to the experts outside your company first? Shift the pattern and start asking your own team members how they would do things differently.

When your boss starts to look outside for good ideas, challenge him or her about where to find best practices. Praise the local talent. Make this a regular conversation at team meetings.

11

There is a gift
in everything.
Can you find it?

Coaching is part of my career. As a counselor and a specialist
in organizational development and change, I have worked
with several hundred executives on an individual basis. As
you might imagine, many of these men and women have told
the stories of their lives and at times their perception was
daunting . . . for them.

I recall one executive—let's call him Rob—whose work life
had become overwhelming, not unusual with today's hectic
pace. In the process of finding quiet time for himself, Rob
had met a woman and the two had had an affair. The affair
had lasted a year. By the time I had begun to work in this
company the affair had come to an end. I soon discovered
that what lingered for Rob was how much he had hurt his
wife.

SHIFT

We began the coaching sessions based on his professional responsibilities in the company. Before long it was very apparent that this affair was still on his mind. Preoccupied with the damage that he thought he had done, he was unable to focus on his professional role. Guilt was the culprit. It was clear that he needed to adopt a different perspective.

As time passed he shared more of his story. Rob loved his wife. He admired her gifts and strengths as a person. He had not meant to hurt her and yet she had been hurt deeply. Nor had he meant to care for another person in the way that he had truly cared for this woman. He was troubled by his actions and the impact they had had on others.

Convinced that he deeply loved his wife, I reminded him that there is a gift in every situation. I knew he could not change what had happened—the past was the past. I knew he *could* change how he thought about the affair and the overall impact on his family life. "Where are the gifts?" I wanted to know. He had some work to do.

Then I asked him about his life and his relationship with his wife prior to his affair. He told me that they had been married for 19 years and that his wife was one of four children. She had been sexually abused as a child and suffered even now because of it. He also noted that she had been a stay-at-home mom and was a truly gifted mother to their two children. He was proud of her and grateful to have such a wonderful wife and mother for his children.

Because she had been at home for so many years she had not built a professional career. Her life's work centered on her children and her ability to provide a home for her family. As a result she was dependent on Rob to provide for her financial and emotional needs. She had never faced the impact of her early abuse and had done little or no work on healing old wounds.

Fraught with guilt, this executive had ended the affair and had eventually told his wife. All he really wanted was to put it all behind him. But his wife was devastated. Now the two were overwhelmed. I took a big-picture approach and encouraged him to see the situation differently. "How has this affair changed your lives for the better?" I asked. "Is there hope for something more?" We agreed that the marriage would never be the same and he noted that it was beginning to improve. We examined the emotional and spiritual gifts that had appeared as a result of his activities outside the marriage.

SHIFT

His wife knew about the affair so he no longer suffered with the tension of hiding it from her. While he knew the other woman was hurt, he had been completely honest with her. His wife, distraught about the situation, had sought a therapist to help her make sense of her life. She was now dealing with her childhood trauma. Rob could see changes in his wife, tiny as they were at the time. He was overjoyed at the possibility of her healing these old wounds. They began therapy as a couple to address the impact that her early abuse had had on their marriage and to release the pain of the affair.

"Why address the intimate aspects of an executive's life?" you might ask. Once again, the best place to start is with our thoughts. So consumed are human beings at times about the inner workings of their lives they simply can't function well. This was the case with Rob. He had taken on a number of new work-related responsibilities with the growth of the business. Each new responsibility had required a high level of concentration and he simply couldn't focus. Not only was he concerned about his marriage but now he was concerned that he was unfit to do the job.

Keep in mind that this was a senior executive who, throughout his professional career, had acquired a great deal of skill.

He was valuable to his company for his technical skill and his strengths as a leader. He no longer felt valuable to himself. The focus of our work together was to have him find the gifts in his life, especially in his marriage. Forgiveness was part of the process—forgiveness of himself. These things he did. Rob is married today. He and his wife are doing well. He remains a powerful leader in his company.

My friend and colleague Louise LeBrun has a wonderful saying. I think it's true. "All decisions are intelligent decisions at the time they are made." The way this man handled his affair resulted in doors opening for him and for all those whose lives he touched. Had he continued to suffer with guilt, those around him would have been impacted by his disdain for himself. He improved his life by practicing the principles of change. Here is what he did.

He started fully where he was within the context of his job and his marriage and he told the truth about what he did and how he felt about his actions. He knew his feelings were affecting his job. He talked about the years prior to the affair and about his boredom with life and his anger at his wife for not dealing with the pain of her abuse.

He acknowledged what was working in his life. He knew he

had a wonderful wife and that on some level he was a very competent executive.

He asked for what he needed and wanted, first, by asking for help to sort out the situation. He also asked for forgiveness from his wife. In doing so he was asking for a new way of looking at his life.

He began to notice how his life was unfolding. As he did this he was able to acknowledge the good things that resulted from the activities in his life, and even that good things had resulted from the affair. He was able to find a sufficient number of gifts that he could turn his life around.

I deeply believe that everything happens for a reason. Growth, painful as it is, requires that we discover new ways to look at the trauma in our lives. There is a gift in everything, and our job is to find the gifts.

EXERCISES

A good time to find the gift at work happens when someone is complaining. All you have to do is acknowledge that they have a point and then ask them, "What might be the gift in this situation?" The question tends to take people off guard a bit so you might preface it with, "I believe there is a positive side to everything." You don't have to push your ideas. Just wait a bit and see what they say.

When you have a bad day ask yourself, "What's the gift here?"

12

How can you measure the intangible?

*The world we have made as a result of the thinking
we have done thus far creates problems that
cannot be solved using the same thinking that
created the situation in the first place.*

Albert Einstein

Chapter 2 outlined new skills required for leadership in our
knowledge-based economy. This entire list of skills is inherent in the human side of change. They are gentler and yet
more powerful in nature than traditional leadership skills.
They help to build relationships. The following list encom-
passes the skills and behaviors that this new leader exhibits.

Declaration:
He declares where he stands. Declaration means that he says
he is going to do something and he does it. Not only does he
do it, he is also seen to do it. Simply stated, he commits.

Silence:

He finds moments to be still. Stillness helps to develop authentic responses and compassion for self and others. The result is an expanded awareness of the big picture. Good leaders know this.

Not knowing:

He suspends his need to have answers. By being silent he creates space for the answers to emerge from within himself and his team.

Listens:

He listens differently. Because he assumes that he does not know what others mean until they tell him, he is able to hear more clearly what they really mean. His communication is superb.

Intuition:

He trusts his own intuition and that of others. He understands the difference between wisdom and intelligence. His intelligence involves business strategics. It's the wisdom of the unconscious mind that guides and directs him.

Flexible:

He is flexible in his leadership style. While he attends to company policy, people are his primary concern and he is interested in creating a situation where they can do their best work.

Authenticity:
His communication is open, authentic, assertive and direct. He says what he means and means what he says. His leadership actions come from his deep sense of purpose and his core values.

Learning:
He encourages individual responsibility for learning. He encourages his staff to identify their own learning needs and go after what they want.

To assess your own leadership skills, see Appendix Four, "Assess Your Profile as a Leader."

Because these skills are intangible, they are difficult to measure. As we know, quantitative measurements don't work well with intangible skills. Qualitative measurements, such as the perception of those who are being led, are more appropriate. Scan the list of leadership skills above. As you do so, consider the kinds of qualitative measurement that might apply for each of the skills mentioned above. These leadership skills are not the norm. New kinds of measurements therefore need to be created.

You might recall from Chapter 1 that qualitative measurements are inherent in people's stories. The stories of staff members help the leader to understand the impact of his leadership style on those whom he leads. Be outrageous. Describe methods of measuring and evidence of success that you might otherwise never consider. Here are a few ideas about gathering qualitative data.

Ask your colleagues to give you feedback on any chosen skills and behaviors from the preceding list. With "declaration," for example, you might say, "It is important to me that I stand by my word. I am working on this and I want to know how people perceive me in this area. Would you be willing to give me some feedback?"

As you practice some of these intangible leadership skills notice whether your team seems more open and responsive at team meetings than they were at previous meetings. Perhaps they are taking greater risks than before. Are they suggesting new and innovative ideas on a more frequent basis? Are they questioning your decisions? All these items are qualitative measurements.

SHIFT

Notice whether you are receiving more accolades from your own boss or from your peers. Do they comment more frequently on your good work? While the comments are qualitative in nature, the frequency constitutes quantitative data.

Does your staff thank you for things that you have done when in the past nothing was mentioned? Is "thank you" becoming more prevalent in your work environment?

Have you or your team been mentioned in the company newsletter lately? The number of mentions could also constitute a quantitative measurement.

Use SMART goal-setting methods. Make sure your goals are specific (S), measurable (M), attainable (A), realistic (R) and trackable (T).

In Chapter 4, I mentioned that Dr. Deming used the concept of Profound Knowledge when he was working with whole-system change. You may also recall that he was a statistician who for much of his professional life worked with numbers, quantitative forms of measurement. During the latter part of his life, however, he emphasized the need to use both quantitative and qualitative data. "Profound Knowledge is a theory," he would say. "It helps you to understand four things, namely, how people think, how people learn, the system in which they work *and* appropriate forms of measurement." The first three items in Profound Knowledge require qualitative measurements.

Then he would add, "The most important things can't be measured, namely, how people think and how they feel." I believe this is true, although some of my technical clients definitely want to measure everything. I remind them that while feelings and thoughts can't be measured, the behavior that results from them can be observed. What we can see, we can also measure. Be clear on what you're measuring. If you can see, touch, taste, smell or hear it, you can probably measure it quantitatively. If you can't, stop trying! It is time to listen and have people tell their story. The stories constitute qualitative measurements.

As people tell their story they change how they feel and how they think. Here is how it works. Qualitative measurements require that you acknowledge people's stories or perceptions about their experience. I use qualitative measurements on a regular basis. In doing so I find that as clients talk about their experience they also release the inner tension that accompanies their negative experiences. When telling their story they begin to recognize that they can influence the outcome. A tiny sense of

---

hope begins to grow. This is triggered by their ability to see how they can influence the outcome in a positive way. They begin to understand how they can change their life. (See Appendix Two for testimonials about qualitative measures.)

All change begins inside. How you view your situation makes all the difference. Start to notice positive behaviors such as more frequent smiles, more positive comments from colleague to colleague, staff and management having lunch together when they formerly did not, and a greater willingness to share ideas about what might improve a situation. These are just a few examples. The rest is up to you.

EXERCISES

How is training and learning handled in your organization? What kinds of things are measured? Are these measurements qualitative or quantitative in nature?

13

What do you think?

When you focus on saving money as a way of
improving quality, costs go up and quality
goes down. When you focus on (serving)
your people as a way of improving quality,
costs go down and quality goes up.
Marvin Weisbord, *Productive Workplaces*

Marvin Weisbord is a consultant in the United States who is
well known for his work in organizational change. His comment above refers to a common business practice in which
the executive team, in times of crisis, tends to pull back on
human resources. They restrict financial spending in all
areas. The company is downsized and managers who implement the day-to-day work find themselves operating as if
their hands are tied. The process of downsizing all by itself
creates a work environment of fear. The thinking of the
executive team is the critical component here. As they think
about saving money, they create the very work environment

127

that they are trying to avoid, one where creativity and innovation disappear, and where quality and timely delivery of
products and services are increasingly difficult.

Back in the 1930s a fellow named Napoleon Hill wrote a book
called *Think and Grow Rich* in which he said, "thoughts are
things." What we think about subsequently becomes our reality. "Notice what you focus on," he reminds the reader,
"because this is what you get." I have noticed over the years
what my executive clients have been thinking about. I can't
read their mind. It shows up in their conversation. What they
think about is exactly what they get.

In the early 1990s I worked extensively with mid-level and
senior executives in the automotive supply industry. I began
to notice that when executives came together in senior team
meetings they spoke of sports, weather and the news. While
they hired Lanny and me to surface the various conflicts in the
company that impacted quality, they themselves rarely spoke
of the real people concerns that they were facing in the company. So one day I asked them to talk about their guiding principles, the ones that governed their actions and behaviors as
company leaders. "What are the norms that you follow around
here? What are the beliefs about leading and managing others?" Here is what they told me.

- "There is one right answer and I had better have it."
- "If things aren't going well, make them look good anyway."
- "Wherever possible use statistics to support your cause."
- "Practice compulsive self-reliance. Don't ask for help. It's a sign of weakness."
- "Talk about change but as much as possible keep the status quo."

It took a while to surface these beliefs and discover how they worked, since none of the executives ever spoke about them. In fact, they did not even know that they shared them. They had simply behaved in ways that suggested to me that these beliefs were happening. These beliefs get in the way. This is how:

- They keep employees from finding creative ways to solve problems.
- They present a false image of the current situation.
- They keep people from asking for the help that they need.
- They minimize innovation and creativity.

Every individual and every team has a set of limiting beliefs. When they are identified and changed, creativity and innovation

SHIFT

increase, as does productivity. Notice how limiting beliefs show up in your company. Do managers and executives ever say that they don't know the answer to something? If they can't say "I don't know what to do here," chances are high that they can't ask for the help that they need. While the limiting belief is invisible, the behavior is noticeable. Whenever you hear a sentence that begins with "I can't do this because . . ." you can be sure there is a limiting belief attached to it.

Limiting beliefs show up in all areas of our life. When we focus on what is possible, then our attitudes and actions start to shift toward what is possible. Attitude is everything. One of my clients pointed this out in his own situation. "I've found that how I think about a problem directly affects my ability to solve it. There have been many times when I did not like the person I was working with and this definitely got in the way of resolution. We, or maybe just I, would focus on what the other person was doing to upset me rather than focusing on the issue." The client's limiting belief was that he believed he was right about his assessment of the other person.

If you want to improve a working relationship then look at your own limiting beliefs about what the other individual can and cannot do. Notice the talent and strength in other people. Help them grow. Ask them what they need in order to develop themselves professionally. Notice each time that you begin a sentence with "We can't do that because . . . ." Offer compliments and support as others progress. Help them do what they do well and what they want to do. Build a support team where people can benefit from each other's ideas and good work. Invite all team members to be part of the process. Address problems that are common to all. Build a common focus and direction. Focus on the end results with members of your team. These are some of the ways to build a better future for yourself, your team and your organization.

If you believe that information is power, you might demonstrate this by holding on to information. The limiting belief is "information is power." If you believe that "sharing what you know in your professional role comes back many times over," then your behavior will be to share what you know. If you believe that "giving to others brings a great working environment to your team," then you are likely to develop a strong work environment for your team. These are powerful beliefs. In fact, when you give to others you invite others to do the same. The team has a tendency to be less tense and more open to new ideas. New ways of working together become apparent. You and your team experience a surge of energy that seems to replenish what you are giving away. Much more comes back to you when you give of yourself.

SHIFT

Stop focusing on what is not working. Practice saying, "Thank you. I really appreciate what you have done."

What we focus on expands and what we resist persists. Notice what you focus on as you travel in to work! Are your thoughts positive or negative? Negative thoughts contribute to negative results. What negative messages are you giving yourself? They need to shift. When you get to work write down just one negative thought and turn it into a positive one. Here is an example.

Limiting thought: There goes the boss favoring Jim again.
Reframe: Jim is a good worker and leader. How can I learn more from him? or How can I help Jim be even greater?

Limiting thought: _____

_____

Reframe: _____

_____

Limiting thought: _____

_____

Reframe: _____

_____

Limiting thought: _____

_____

Reframe: _____

_____

Limiting thought: _____

_____

Reframe: _____

_____

Section IV

Ask for What You Want
and Need

»Shift happened

14

New techniques are more effective.

If you want a plan implemented, a company organized, work redesigned, or many problems solved all at once, get as many key stakeholders as possible in one room and ask them to work on the task together. Use a wide-angle lens. Reaffirm dignity. Help people find meaning in their work. Move toward your vision of community in the workplace. It's certainly not the "one best way" . . . [it's] quite simply the only way.

Marvin Weisbord, *Productive Workplaces*

In this quotation Weisbord refers to the need to involve all stakeholders at the same time in order to create a groundswell of passion for the company direction and for desired organizational change. While this change technique is not the norm for addressing a company's challenge, there are exceptions. During my years in Michigan I worked in high-tech industries. In the following situation one of our clients, a manager, refers to bringing the entire group of stakeholders together.

During release our business managers were under extreme pressure to deliver our product to our customer. Up to this point they were provided inaccurate information about our progress. I became the project prime, explained to them the truth and worked with all of them and our customer to find the best way out so that we could all meet our business objectives. It was the painful truth that made everyone wake up and smell the coffee and figure out how to get out of the mess. While I wasn't fully sure about how to get out of the mess, I sure knew we had to own up to it. (See Chapter 5 for more on telling the truth.)

I also worked with companies where tradition was the norm. In one case I found myself at the front end of change with a huge unionized automotive supplier. The senior management team was working closely with the senior union leaders. Both groups supported this program. Their collective purpose was to implement a system-wide employee involvement program to improve quality. While the program offered solid training material, the union membership did not accept it. Management's attempt to cascade the program downward throughout the entire company was resisted. Regardless of their approach, the action and intentions of management were seen as one form of top-down authoritarian management after another.

Management described the situation as one where "the union membership does not want to change." "They actually resist change," the leaders told us. "We get to a certain point in the process and we can almost palpate the resistance. Union members simply don't want to change." The union leaders corroborated this statement.

My curiosity was sufficiently high that I wanted to hear the union members' perspective. I wandered into the cafeteria and spent a good part of the day talking with union folks. "How do you respond to change?" I asked them. Here is what they told me.

"We have had five general managers in the plant over the past six years. Each wanted to reorganize and so they did just that. We had to adjust to new procedures and new operating methods with each manager. Change is constant here. Our resistance is not so much to change as it is to authoritarian leadership." Perhaps this scenario sounds familiar.

One group after another told similar stories. "We want

recognition for our contribution and our management doesn't seem to want to listen. More than anything, we want to share what we know. When something doesn't work on the shop floor, guess who's there! We are. We want to be asked about what we need and what we don't need around here. We're used to change; we've been at it for a number of years. We want to be heard when it comes to improving things," they told me. "What we don't like is that no one asks us what is needed and we're the ones who do the work. We're the ones who know."

All they really wanted was to be invited to be part of the enterprise, to share their ideas and to know they were being heard. In fact they knew intimately what contributed to high and low levels of quality. They had seen how things worked in the process of designing, building and delivering the product. New methods of leading were needed. Management and union together needed to learn to shift the power from the top of the organization to lower levels where implementation happened. New leadership thinking was required. The union members were eager.

In this situation employees wanted to talk about what they knew, yet they were never asked. After several failed attempts to say what they wanted and needed in order to keep quality levels high, they felt that their input was unwelcome. Steeped in the need to mobilize fast-moving quality improvement, the leaders weren't open to hearing what was really needed. In fact, the leaders had been trained to believe that they themselves "should" know how to make things happen. It never occurred to them to ask for help. Without direct and early involvement on the part of the workforce in the change process, as with this quality initiative program, resistance was predictable. What was needed was to "invite" the workforce to be part of the quality program.

The situation with Harold was similar. It was one where new techniques in managing human direction, energy and passion were needed. Harold was a manager with a highly committed team, one where the attrition rate was very low. Most of Harold's team had worked with him for several years; this was unusual in the high-tech environment. Harold noticed increasing numbers of product revisions that his team, mainly engineers, were responsible for. "Their job is to find the problems so that's what they do," he told me. "The trouble is that they are paid to find the problems and when they find the problems they then have to solve the problems. They never get out of this loop."

Harold was right. A team cannot move forward when they are

SHIFT

rewarded for finding problems and they are paid to focus on problems that were created in the past. When a team focuses on solving the problems at hand they invariably find them linked to other problems. The resolution of one problem leads to another and there seems to be no end. Forward movement is essential. A different approach is required. In his frustration Harold outlined a classic situation. "I am dealing with engineers," he told me, "and engineers are trained to do a root cause analysis. We now have over 2,000 problems to correct and the focus is still on finding problems." They need to get past problem solving and into creating the next phase of the work.

The moral of the story, and the new technique in management, is this. Don't focus on problem solving. Something else is needed, namely, to create a shared direction or vision. As deeper, yet related problems begin to surface, team members and clients find themselves engulfed in the very problems they are trying to correct. My suggestion over the years has been to stop the bleeding, so to speak, and to turn to new ways of resolving the situation. The answer lies in focusing rather than fixing (see Chapter 15 for more on focusing).

"So what's the new technique?" you might ask. I mention Harold's situation only to point out that old ways of making change by using problem-solving techniques are no longer effective. In both his situation and that of the large automotive supplier at the beginning of this chapter, there is a useful and similar approach. Involve as many stakeholders as possible at the same time. Create a groundswell for change. Help people talk openly with one another. Include those at the top, those in the middle, and as many of the front-line employees as possible in the same meeting. When you do this, collaboration, responsibility, accountability and innovation are all addressed at one time. It's not the best way, as Weisbord says; it's the only way.

EXERCISES

Recall for a moment some of the problem-solving techniques and root-cause analysis exercises that you initiated over the years. What happened to the problems? How did the situation get resolved? Did it ever get resolved?

Identify a current problem in the workplace. Stop trying to solve it yourself. Bring as many stakeholders into the room as possible and have them address the situation in the presence of each other. Notice how people engage in resolving the situation. Speak about the problem as if it has already been resolved. Write it down in the present tense and speak about

SHIFT

the positive only. Stay clear of negative comments such as "I don't want any more problems to appear," and shift to "All our problems have been important to us. They are now a thing of the past" or "Any challenges we experience are resolved effortlessly as we use the collective mindset of all those concerned to move forward."

15

Remember where you're going!

You have noticed repeatedly by now that how we think is an essential part of creating what we want in our life. Our thoughts guide our conversations and ultimately they guide our actions. Perhaps North Americans don't notice this link between the power of thought and the creation of our future. Take a look at your job, for example, and think of a situation that you believe could be improved. You can begin these improvements by conducting a visioning exercise. Here is how it works.

Imagine that you are talking with colleagues about a situation that needs improving. As you talk to them, describe the situation as if it were now in perfect order. Describe the situation in as much detail as you can think of. All the improvements that you have ever thought possible have actually happened. Notice the thoughts you have about this new situation and write them down. From the moment that you start to define this future situation in your mind, it is important to use the *present tense*.

SHIFT

When you use the present tense, as if the situation has already happened, the process is hastened. This technique of imagining the future as if it has already happened is called visioning.

When you focus on the end result, that is what you create. For more on this see Chapter 16, "If you want it, you create it!" As you define this "future state," resist describing the action steps. There is a reason for this. When you focus on how to proceed, you are beginning a problem-solving technique, and more problems show up. As you have seen in Chapter 14, leave problem solving behind. Otherwise you risk unintentionally creating more problems.

Sometimes you have to deal with the immediate problem long enough to resolve a crisis—metaphorically speaking, to stop the bleeding. Then continue with the new approach. When you use the present tense, your subconscious mind acts as if the situation has already happened. Your language shifts so that other people hear you talking about your direction with certainty. They also hear you speak as if the future was already happening. For example, you might say "My VP really listens (present tense) when I tell her about a problem." In reality she may not be doing this at all. Not to worry. The activity here is to define the situation as you want it to be, as if it were already happening.

As you focus on a future state, with your boss, for example, you notice that you are thinking about her in a more positive light. You build a positive expectation about her interactions with you. As you think of her in positive ways you automatically, unconsciously, begin to treat her better, often without even noticing your behavior. While no words are spoken, something changes inside of you and your boss. The picture you hold is in the future state and the language you use is in the present tense. Both of these techniques used simultaneously work to suggest that your boss is important in your life. While no words are spoken, something changes—your thoughts, for one thing. Your boss and others pick up subtle shifts in your behavior, perhaps without your ever saying a word. Your boss may sense that you are treating her in more caring ways. The chance of her responding positively is huge. As you change the focus of your intention to focus on the positive side of your boss, others begin to notice changes in you. What you focus your attention on expands. Make sure what you think about is what you really want because that's what you're going to get.

Visioning is a great technique. It can be used individually to plan your life or it can be used to create a common direction for a whole team. Remember, when using it for the whole team, to include from the beginning the ideas of all those who

SHIFT

will ultimately be part of the solution. Use the techniques of brainstorming to get everyone's ideas on the table. These techniques include the following:

- Quantity here is more important than quality.
- There is no discussion or dialogue about whether someone's ideas are appropriate.
- Participants do not question each other during the brainstorm.
- Silence is okay.
- Piggybacking on another's idea is okay.
- Have one person write all the comments on a flip chart during the brainstorm.

Not long ago I was talking with a manager about the power of visioning and he remembered the following story.

Back in the UK I worked on a telecom product for the UK market. At the time we were only mildly successful, with a small customer base in the UK, but there were signs that British Telecom and some major European vendors were coming on board. We knew it would affect our day-to-day business enormously. Our management gathered all the lower management together to go through the Process of Management Tool. It was great. First we defined a purpose, then a shared vision, then core values and then an action plan to achieve our vision. It was clear from the beginning that when important decisions were to be made we would reflect on our vision to help us set our priorities. It was an example that we can work at web speed without being too chaotic. I just want to point out one thing, Janice. We do not have a vision, let alone a shared vision, in the company that I am with today. As a result we are chaotic and we can't make timely decisions.

This fellow had the right idea and had connected it to his work in the UK. He was right about the company he was in. Fortunately we were in the early stages of a whole-system change process. We still had a lot of work to do. We knew what needed to be done and the vision was on its way.

EXERCISES

Using the present tense and pushing out in time about a year from now, create a vision for your relationship with your manager. Imagine that your working relationship with each other is great. Describe what it looks like in writing. During quiet moments read your notes every day for the next two weeks. Create your "desired future" by focusing on it.

Using the present tense and pushing out in time about a year

SHIFT

from now, create a vision for your relationship with your team. Begin with "It's now _____" (six months into the future). Imagine that your working relationships within the team are great. Describe in writing what this looks like and how people are behaving and responding. Once again choose a quiet moment to read your notes daily over the next two weeks.

On a separate page write these two partial sentences, one on the left at the top of the page and one on the right:

"My boss would be perfect if she or he _____"
"Things would be great around here if _____"

Complete each sentence with as many ideas as you can imagine about what a perfect end result would look like. Quantity is more important than quality so fill the page! Use the rules of brainstorming from this chapter.

What does a vision of leadership look like for you? Imagine the situation. See in your mind the result as you want it to be. Begin with a broad image and watch it begin to take shape over the next few weeks. Write it down. Add details. Then begin to see how your vision is actually starting to materialize. What are you noticing on a daily basis? Pay attention to what you focus on, because that is what you will get.

16

If you want it,
you create it!

Whatever you notice, you are inviting into your life.
Whatever you talk about, you are inviting into your
life. Whatever you identify with in your thoughts,
words and actions, you are inviting into your life.
Catherine Ponder, *Open Your Mind to Receive*

You have the power to create what you want in your life. First
you think about what you want and then you ask for what you
want. The words you use are critical. Pay attention to your
language and make sure that you focus on what you want—
and nothing else.

Creating what you want means bringing to life in concrete
ways the things that you think about. All change, all plans, our
lifestyles, vacations, spouses, career promotions, new houses
or cars and even friendships are created first in our thoughts.
The motto for Disney World is a perfect example: "If you

dream it, it can happen." Pay attention to your thoughts because that's what you will create in your life.

By now you might be tired of hearing this message repeatedly; however, I'll say it again. The most significant breakthroughs in our life all begin inside of us. Here are the steps involved.

Think about what you want. Let's make it a new computer.

Talk about it with a friend or colleague who knows something about computers. As you talk with people, the word spreads to others that you need a computer, perhaps a specific kind of computer. Those who can contribute to your need start to respond. Your database of information grows.

Act on what you want. Read the "for sale" columns in the paper. In this case the conversations in fact are the actions that need to take place. Be specific, speak in the present tense and entertain all ideas.

Before long you will find yourself connected with people who can find the computer that you want. Thought, word and action—that's how it happens. It's simple. Our culture is not used to noticing this simple order of things. We tend to try so hard to make something happen that we get in the way of it happening. We complicate the process.

Here are a few hints to hasten the process of creating what you want.

Thinking about what you want repeatedly helps to make it happen. Pay attention to what you think you want.

Writing on paper the things that you want reinforces the second step, which is talking about what you want and need. Writing thoughts down or talking about them to someone else helps you to get the thoughts outside of your mind. They then become part of another person's thoughts.

The language you use is important because it hastens or slows the process of change. Using positive language such as "My senior manager is really interested in helping me grow" creates synergy between your manager and yourself. A positive relationship has a chance to grow. Negative language works in reverse; therefore, use positive language.

Our innermost thoughts affect our behavior when we are with others, our leader included. The manager gets the message without our saying that we really don't believe we will receive that promotion. The rest you know. Change the way you think!

Whenever and wherever you can, take action.

Our experiences and our language actually cause physical responses in our body. They shape our thinking. A high-tech client of mine described it by saying, "We are hard-wired to respond in certain ways." He's right. He was referring to words like "boss," "timelines," "product release" and a variety of words in his industry. When you hear a favorite piece of music, what kind of response happens in your belly, in your arms or in your chest? If you were a teenager in the 1960s, as I was, rock and roll might bring a physical response and get you moving even today. I still experience a rush of adrenalin when I hear Natalie Cole sing or Gerry Mulligan play his saxophone. I am hard-wired, or perhaps just programmed, to love jazz. Other people love blues, classical or western music. If you find these ideas interesting you can learn a great deal more about them through programs on Neurolinguistic Programming (NLP). See Louise LeBrun's *Fully Alive From 9 to 5* in the Bibliography at the end of this book. Search the Internet for books on NLP and check your local community colleges for NLP programs. Most large cities in Canada and the United States offer these programs.

Karen is an example of a company executive who created what she wanted. She had been in a leadership role for over two years. She was good at her job and knew it well. She was also unhappy in her job and wasn't sure why. Karen knew she needed a change and lacked the enthusiasm to push herself forward. As a loyal employee for 20 years she tended to follow corporate rules and regulations. She contacted me to help her grow professionally.

While Karen was quite creative in how she approached her life, she held a lid on her creativity at work. Karen worked with a number of very conservative leaders and was concerned about rocking the boat. She wanted to fit in, and in an effort to maintain the status quo she had blocked herself from growing. It was no surprise to me that she felt stagnant and bored and that these feelings were impacting other parts of her life. Her social life had dwindled, work lacked challenge, family meals had become uninteresting and she had a vague sense of anxiety most of the time. All of these, by the way, are signs of mild depression. Karen really needed a change.

Here is what happened. We worked on a vision for her work and her life. She learned to ask herself and others for what she really wanted. She began with the first principle of change: "Start fully where you are and tell your truth." She had to acknowledge that she was not happy in her job and at the same time she had to be specific about why. She acknowledged what was working in her job and then decided what she wanted and needed in order to be happy and feel fulfilled. This last item was a bit more difficult because she was used to following the rules and doing her job in the way that she saw others behave. But once these steps were in place, the next ones appeared.

She thought about what she wanted in her life. She started with a general image, then she went on to specifics. When she wasn't sure she made it up.

She changed her thoughts about work. This step was critical for her. She wanted to improve her work and her work environment. She had to ask herself, "If this were the perfect job for me, how would it look, and what would I be saying and doing?" She had to get used to using the present tense as if her thoughts had already happened.

She paid attention to her language. Was it negative or positive? She had to know. When she heard the doubt in her comments she had to create a positive spin. Instead of saying, "We tried that last year and there was no change," or "Nothing moves around here," she found herself saying: "We tried that last year. However, the circumstances are different now and it may very well work," and "A few things have changed for the better around here." As she changed negative language and thoughts to positive ones she began to have positive experiences.

Until this time Karen hadn't given much thought to her own "inner scripts" about accepting her life as it was. She knew she needed to change but she didn't know where to begin. Through coaching, she learned to use positive statements to create the job that she wanted. In doing so she created the following vision for herself. Here is what she wrote.

It is now 18 months into the future (she named the date).
- I am working with a new group of innovative people.
- I am earning 25 percent more.
- I am influencing my colleagues in very positive ways.
- I am highly creative in my work and am recognized for my creativity.
- My boss acknowledges my good work.
- I begin and end my day with great enthusiasm.
- I am in line for another promotion.
- My work and my life are exciting.
- I am proud of my good work.

SHIFT

Changes began to happen, small ones at first. As Karen changed her leadership role, her life followed suit. If you're ready, you can do it too.

EXERCISES

Once you have identified what you want, write it down! List a dozen things you could do to make it happen. Small steps are great. Choose one idea to act on. Talk about it with a few colleagues. Take the next step and act on it! Notice how you feel.

Each day notice what you have done to meet your goal. Regularly notice changes that suggest your goals are coming about. The tiny changes eventually become huge.

17

Partnering is
where it's at.

In most lives insight has been accidental . . .
but making mental connections is our most crucial
learning tool, the essence of human intelligence
—to forge links; to go beyond the given; to
see patterns, relationships, context.
Marilyn Ferguson, *The Aquarian Conspiracy*

For me, partnering with others is a way of life. I have noticed that many of the people I meet have values and beliefs similar to my own. Some of them even think like me. I meet them in different walks of life, in client organizations, in theater line-ups, on planes and in my own neighborhood. They may work in a different profession and some live in different cities.

In *The Aquarian Conspiracy*, Marilyn Ferguson observes this phenomenon and links it to a shift in thinking that is taking place. "We are drawn to each other," says she, "from many walks of life because we share a passion for something different, something that is changing our lives." This something is a "new way of thinking" and it's shaping our world.

This difference in thinking shows up in our workplaces in a popular leadership instrument called the Myers Briggs Temperament Inventory (MBTI). In its shorter form it's known as the Kiersey Sorter. Basically it's a psychological instrument that defines several tendencies of leadership. I use this instrument to help executives understand a bit more about themselves, accept the diversity on their team and make greater sense of this global shift in thinking.

The instrument describes eight different traits of leadership, in sixteen different combinations. The combination of extroversion, sensing, thinking and judgment (ESTJ), for example, is one that has grown our economy. These particular four traits have contributed to such things as the development of a healthy national economy, a solid business direction for manufacturing and the business world, financial growth, and a sense of order in politics and society in the western world. The traits of the ESTJ are particularly important because they tend to stabilize a system or an organization. They are also known to create policy and to support existing policy.

On the other hand, the combination of the four leadership traits of introversion, intuition, feeling and perception (INFP) is drawing us forward into a new way of thinking. Leaders with this profile are highly creative, introspective, compassionate and intuitive. They are curious and have the capacity to live with greater degrees of uncertainty and chaos.

Of the sixteen possible combinations of leadership traits, the ESTJ and the INFP represent poles opposite to each other. One type is neither better nor worse than the other. They are simply different.

If we expect forward movement of our culture to occur with either the ESTJ on its own or the INFP on its own, we will be disappointed. The one set of traits, ESTJ, is steeped in tradition. It focuses on stability and order and maintains predictability; it requires the INFP to help move it forward. The other set of traits, the INFP, is highly creative and innovative. It looks toward the future, creating possibilities. It requires the structure and discipline of the ESTJ to move the culture forward. More than any other time in history we now need the combination of all eight leadership traits (extrovert, introvert, sensing, intuition, thinking, feeling, judgment and perception).

SHIFT

These two poles, the ESTJ and the INFP, are important because they represent the extremes of cultures that we are adjusting to. The one, ESTJ, is the traditional, top-down hierarchical culture that is so strongly represented in institutions such as government, health care, education and many religions. The other, INFP, (introversion, intuition, feeling, perception), is the emerging collaborative culture that shows up in high-tech start-up industries, in the plethora of small businesses that have emerged and in the creative arts, to name only a few.

Let me share a bit about "making mental connections," which Marilyn Ferguson refers to in the opening quotation of this chapter. I am an ENFP (extroversion, intuition, feeling, perception) which, according to statistics, is represented in about 5 percent of the general population. That means there are five ENFP's in every hundred people in the general population. There are 13 (13%) ESTJ's in the general population. The 13 other combinations are represented by various percentages between the three I mentioned. The point I am making is this. The chances of my meeting other ENFP's is five in a hundred, not too high. Nevertheless, senior executives and a variety of other managers whose profile is similar to my own contact me. They are often ready to make major changes in their organization and they know I can help them move forward.

We are drawn to each other in ways that we can't see.

Developing new thoughts and new leadership skills requires that you pay close attention to "how things happen." Partnering is key. Start to notice the new people you meet. Do they share the beliefs and values that you hold dear?

EXERCISES

Make connections with other people, especially if they are not part of your immediate work group. Notice the traits and characteristics that are similar to yours and those that are not. Consider how you might work on a joint project with another person by having them as a partner on that project. What would you want to know about them in order to have a good partnership experience?

Review your Myers Briggs Temperament Inventory (MBTI) on the Internet. Start to talk with people who know something about their own MBTI profile. Learn about the different pairs of leadership traits and especially learn about your own traits and how they impact on others. There are many other good leadership profiles on the market. Find them and use what works for you.

Section V

Step Aside and Notice
What Is Changing

»Shift continues to happen

18

Let go of your attachment to the outcome.

Discoveries and theories of new science called me . . .
to a vision of the inherent orderliness of the universe,
of creative processes and dynamic, continuous change
that still maintained order . . . a world where order
and change, autonomy and control were not the great
opposites that we had thought them to be. It was a
world where change and constant creation signaled
new ways of maintaining order and structure.
Margaret Wheatley, author and Harvard professor

Control is the big issue here. The only control we ever really have is over ourselves. So often when working with a senior executive group I find that they have decided on their direction; each step is clearly defined. Their planning happens at a management retreat or at an off-site meeting. There is nothing inherently wrong in this. But something gets in their way and

SHIFT

keeps their well-laid strategies from realization. What is that thing? They have decided in advance what each step "should" look like, and in today's business culture change happens quickly. A step-by-step plan can change overnight; in fact it often does, especially in the high-tech business world.

A few years ago I had occasion to speak with a man who was responsible for finding the majority of venture capital funding for many of the start-up companies in his city. He was also a seasoned engineer and a well-respected businessman. We talked about some of the issues for managers in the high-tech sector and the importance of managers understanding themselves. We were talking about transformational change and the management growth that is required to create and sustain business changes. He stopped me at one point and said, "Janice, I don't understand everything you do but I know we need your skills in this town." When I asked him to explain why, he simply said, "Because in the high-tech world we start up overnight and we die overnight." All of you are familiar with at least one company that has suffered this fate.

Changes in the high-tech world are happening so fast that we can hardly keep up. When there is a problem with equipment the company sends in a team to correct it. This is not the case for management. If a team is having problems the manager is expected to figure it out. And yet his or her team consists of human beings, which require a different set of skills to manage than does equipment or products or technology. If the manager is good with people, the team moves forward. If he is not, the stress increases, and quality, timely delivery of products and services, and customer satisfaction are at stake. When change happens overnight there are lessons that must be learned. I discovered over the years that even when the product and technology of a company are sound, their methods of managing their people often are not. Companies grow when their employees are cared for and when they have a say in the direction of the company. They commit when they share their voice.

The Buddhists have a practice that might be helpful here. It's called the Four-Fold Path. The process requires that four simple steps be used in daily practice. While they are incredibly simple they are also difficult to follow. Our need to control next steps gets in the way. The Four-Fold Path requires that you:

- Show up;
- Pay attention;
- Tell the truth;
- Let go of your attachment to the outcome.

SHIFT

Have a look at these in the context of your leadership role. Let's say you're attending a meeting in your director's office. You have to get to the meeting before you can be part of the meeting. Therefore, the first step for you is to show up. It's that simple, just be present and arrive at the beginning of the meeting. Think of the number of people who arrive late for meetings. When we arrive late it is more difficult to pay attention and be present to what is happening. We may need to ask questions about what has already taken place and often the meeting time is stretched because of this.

The second step is to pay attention. There are a few parts to this. First, it means to pay attention to what is happening in the room. Who is present? What is happening? How are various messages being conveyed? What is the content of the meeting? Who is saying what? It also means to pay attention to your own thoughts. What is going on inside you? Are you resisting what is being said? Are you drawn to sounds outside the room? Paying attention means to be attentive to the inner aspect of yourself as well as to the events that are happening in your immediate surroundings. It also means being present to the conversation at hand so that you can be engaged in the meeting.

The third step is to tell the truth. The thing to keep in mind here is to tell your own truth. It's the only truth you really know. The truth comes out of a willingness first to show up and then to be present in the ways mentioned above.

The final step is to let go of your attachment to the outcome. In our North American culture this is the most difficult step. Human beings have a tendency to form attachments to most things. We form attachments to people; we become aware of this when we realize that we prefer one to another. We form attachments to clothes; we prefer one suit or pair of shoes to another. We form attachments to our car; we prefer a Cadillac, Pontiac, Volvo, Acura or Ferrari. We form attachments to the outcomes of meetings before the meeting actually begins by lining up in our mind what we want to have happen. When we are fixed on how things should, must or ought to happen we are no longer able to let the "best way" appear.

In the world of business this last item plays havoc. Fixed on one way of succeeding, we can't see another; and the other method may surpass the first in profit, in efficiency and in a number of other ways. Invariably when I work with executive or management teams they discover a better way. It always requires that they let go of attachment to the one right way that they were committed to have happen.

Letting go of attachment requires trust. At the moment I am

thinking about selling my house. I don't yet know where I want to move to and I keep pushing myself to make this decision. I look in one community and then another and realize that the decision about where to move to is not yet made. To accomplish this last step in the four-fold way I could let go of having to have an answer and ask my subconscious mind to allow this next step to appear. The moment I get my decision making out of the way the answer will appear. I have done this enough in my life on my own and with clients to know that the process works, and still I get in the way. It's part of being human. For you it may be part of beginning a different method of planning your future:

- let go of *what* you think should happen;
- let go of *how* you think things should happen;
- notice what actually happens.

This is what letting go of attachment is all about.

EXERCISES

If you are the leader and responsible for completing a certain project, notice how you work to make that project happen. What techniques do you use to keep the project rolling? Do you feel that you have to push people? Can you get out of the way and let your people decide on the best way to reach the goal?

Try working with your team to have them identify a common direction. Write it on a flip chart and have your team list several methods to reach that direction. Now have them vote on the top four methods. How will you deal with their choices if they are not the same choices that you would make? Notice your attachment to how you think things should happen.

Notice what is getting in the way of a smoothly functioning team. Are you thinking, "I'm the boss and should know what to do here," or "If I don't direct this thing people will think I don't know what to do"? There are many choices here. What are the thoughts that get in your way in a situation like this?

19

Silent time is valuable time.

Chapter 2 outlined emerging skills of leadership, among them the need to be still. Imagine—a useful and important leadership skill for a leader today is to be still! I noted that the tendency of the human mind is to be busy during all its conscious waking moments. Something deep inside drives people today to be busy, and yet, new thought comes into our awareness when we are silent. If we want to be creative and innovative we must rely on our mind to come up with new ideas, and yet, in the work environment being still is considered to be counter-productive. It is equated with being idle.

But stillness and idleness are not the same. Being idle usually means "not productive" and "lazy." Being still offers moments for the mind and for the body to re-energize. When being still becomes a practice, new ideas and creativity emerge. Innovative business practices come from this.

With the pace and demands of running a business, leaders require the ability to concentrate and to take clear direction and purposeful decisions. Being still helps to access this ability. Deep and meaningful change comes in quiet moments when we are not distracted and when we are free from the "shoulds" of leadership roles and work-related responsibilities.

If you are in a leadership role, can you find time to be still and to quiet your busy mind for a short time each day? Being silent allows you to look inside for what you need. When you sit still you force yourself to slow down. Your mind becomes clear. When you sit still and breathe deeply you can focus your attention on your breathing alone. Clarity of thought appears; new ideas surface; resolution of long-standing problems shows up. Running doesn't help you reach your destination any faster. The very act of slowing down allows you to become more creative, more innovative and more efficient. You may have to slow down to speed up.

My family offers a picture of the pace of modern-day life. Rebecca, my daughter, is ambitious and off to pursue a second postgraduate degree. She and my son-in-law, Russell, are living in London, England, for a year while Rebecca attends the London School of Economics. They live in Wimbledon, just outside the core of London itself. During one of my visits to

SHIFT

the UK, Russell commented on their lifestyle in the great city of London. "It takes so much energy to live here, Janice." The two of us engaged in a long conversation about life in London compared to life in Ottawa. We talked about the details of his hectic life in England. Here is what he told me.

Russell gets up at five in the morning, goes through his morning routines like the rest of us, leaves the house at six and rushes to the train. At this early hour many people in their neighborhood are also rushing to the train. Each one lines up with their "subway face" to get a train ticket or to pass through the turnstile for the London "tube." People are hustling everywhere; they are pushing to find a seat and often, even at this early hour, the train is full—standing room only becomes the norm. Cellphones appear. As the train pulls out several passengers call their offices. They leave messages for themselves about what to remember as their day proceeds. "The train is anything but quiet," Russell reminds me. "I had hoped to find a few minutes to focus on my day, even just to read a bit. No such luck."

His train pulls into Waterloo Station. The crowd leans on the exit doors. Russell is bumped and shoved along with everyone else as they leave the train. The station is packed with people rushing and he is racing through the crowd for the tube. Those of you who have traveled on the London tube can recall the maze of underground tunnels that lead from one subway train to the next. As he runs along, Russell is aware of the "energy" that propels the crowd—he is part of it, moving faster, noticing his watch and thinking about the day ahead. He is organizing his day, lining up meeting after meeting and wondering how he will juggle various projects and fit in brief conversations with others—all activities in a hectic, yet meaningful, workday. Russell was speaking for many of us when he told his story. He assured me that in London the pace and stress of life was extreme.

Each of us needs to re-energize. Being still helps this happen. However, life in large international cities—New York, Hong Kong, Mexico City, Athens, Chicago and even Toronto on a lesser scale—have that familiar frenetic pace of London. In our increasingly fast-paced lives there are fewer moments of quiet. Culture surrounds us with fast-moving traffic, radio reports, impatient drivers, constantly increasing methods of electronic communication, more people and demands of one sort or another—all this before we get to work. Media bombards our space; chatter in our mind is endless. Computers, technology and new electronic gadgets fill our workspace.

SHIFT

At home the story is similar—new kitchen appliances, a television in every room, woofers, 300 cable stations, electronic toys and so on. Adding to the pace, we change our car, our home, our computer, clothes, friends, city and sometimes even our spouse on a regular basis.

If you are managing people or you're in a leadership role you're probably experiencing all of this. How to survive is a significant question. The unspoken message and invisible programming that accompanies this pace in our lives is "keep producing, go faster, work harder, don't stop." There is no legitimate downtime for people to nourish their mind, their body and their spirit. This is especially true for people in leadership roles.

With little attention paid to the frantic pace, we risk illness. If we don't care for ourselves, we die. Slowing down allows us to go inside and discover what is really important. Remember that all change begins within. If we are to care for our families, our friends, our employees and others, we must also care for ourselves. How do we stop or slow this frenetic pace? At the top of my list is the need to be still and slow the frenetic mind.

Let's look at the value of being still. Slowing down is key. Good things happen to the body when we keep it still. Blood pressure and the immune system stabilize. Communicative diseases such as viruses and the common cold are less likely to take hold. Heart rate and breathing slow down. The cells of the body are nourished. Creativity and innovation expand. Physical health improves. Productivity at work increases. Quality of life is enhanced. Quality production and quality service improve. These are only a few.

A leader's work requires that he create meaning for his organization. He can only do that when he himself is clear. To gain the most from employees show them how this is done. Care for yourself! Be the best you can be! Bring balance and clarity of thought! Plan your work to include quiet time! Twenty minutes daily throughout your week replenishes your spirit. When you care for yourself you model what you want of others, to have them slow down and care for themselves as well. Everyone benefits.

EXERCISES

Notice how you push yourself faster and faster through daily routines. Take some time right now to identify how you do this.

SHIFT

Do you have a cellphone? If yes, how many people have your number? What can you do to limit the incoming calls so that you can spend quality time with yourself?

Building quality silent time for yourself requires thoughtfulness. Take time at the beginning of your day to meditate. Before going in to your office, sit in your car and listen to Mozart. At the end of either of these activities make a mental note of a few ways to slow down during your day's work. Speak more slowly, write, walk and eat more slowly. All of these things slow the pace but not the efficiency of your work.

When an executive tells me he is operating at 200 percent I know he is not efficient. We only have 100 percent of our time to give. Anything else is out of control. What are your patterns when you are at work? Do you leave space between meetings to replenish your energy? Do you race from one meeting to the next? Take a guess at your level of effectiveness when you do this. Is it 70 percent, perhaps even less? This racing may cost you your life. It certainly costs your company plenty in terms of lack of productivity.

What is the quality of your leisure time? How do you actually spend your time? When you are at home in the evening, for example, do you listen to the radio, watch TV, read, play with

your children, converse with your partner, walk in your neighborhood, work in your garden, exercise? When you pay attention to these things you grow old with grace, and you know
your life is worthwhile. Consider the alternative—when you
don't pay attention to these things, you grow old feeling
unfulfilled.

Perhaps this is a strange thought, but—how do you bring
leisure to work? (See *It's Not About Time* by Joe Pavelka in
the Bibliography at the end of this book.)

Chapter 20

Noticing tiny steps actually builds the culture.

By now you are probably familiar with the idea that, as a leader, how you think is everything. All changes in an organization begin first with how people think. Their willingness to act is heavily dependent on the company norms, especially on the openness of the culture to have its people take risks. To assess this I generally ask the question, "How does your culture deal with mistakes?" When mistakes are celebrated as an opportunity to grow, the level of safety and the ability to take risks grows.

After working with executives and their teams for the better part of 18 years, I have come to believe that what managers, senior managers and executives really want is to make improvements in their work and their workplace. This helps to keep their customers happy. Their specific use of language creates their organizational culture and it either hastens or deters their goals from happening. I am not suggesting that executives get up in the morning thinking, "I'm going in to work to see what destruction I can cause." Nor do they notice the impact of their language on the world that they spend one third of their lives in, their organization. Executives actually create the culture by the way they use language in their organization. While they may not be the ones to initiate the particular conversations that take place, they do keep alive the way things have always happened in their culture. Here are a few ways in which they perpetuate the culture by using the language that they do:

A production manager says to his team, "I am not sure we can get this number out the door, but let's try to do it." The fact that he started the comment with "I'm not sure . . . " leaves his team doubting the possibility. His language builds the doubt. Also, there is no commitment in the word "try." "Let's do it" is much stronger and invites involvement.

The CEO focuses on the competition's forward movement. He announces his concern to his entire company. Employees throughout the company begin to focus on how well the competition is doing. "Does this mean we are not doing so well?" they wonder. The principle to remember is this: "What we focus on expands." The CEO may have inadvertently contributed to the competition doing well by focusing on their

SHIFT

results instead of his own company's results. By sending the message that he did, his language and his focus may have contributed to the situation that he wanted to avoid.

Notice how your mission statement is worded. Does it begin with "We will provide top-quality service, etc."? When a mission statement is set in the future tense the subtle message that is received by those hearing or reading it is that this mission will happen in the future. Hopefully the company leaders want the message to be true in the moment that it is read, not in the future. It is much more powerful to use the present tense in the mission statement—as if the company is already the best. Say instead "We provide top-quality service." Those around you will hear the difference in your language and respond to it as if the statement "we are the biggest and the best" were already true. When clients hear the present tense they are more likely to choose you to do the work for them.

Change is constant. What we think about is what we create in our lives. While change actually begins with an executive's thinking, the language he uses helps to make it happens. His use of language conditions his entire work culture to think and behave in certain ways. Notice what you think about in your leadership role. What do you talk about with colleagues and direct reports? Most importantly, is your message framed in a positive way? And remember to tell the truth.

A culture's ability to celebrate plays a role in fulfilling the mission statement. Have a look at how this works in your organization. The following questions are important because the answers will give you an idea about what the culture focuses on, and what it focuses on is what it gets. Language makes it happen.

- Do you focus on success?
- Does your team celebrate on a daily basis?
- How is the idea of success developed?
- Are you preoccupied with the things that aren't working?
- What does success look, sound and feel like for your team?
- Is there agreement among your team members about what constitutes success?
- Is success measured mainly in terms of numbers?
- Does success include people's feelings of pride, recognition and self-satisfaction?

Remember, what you focus on is what you get, so pay attention to what you and your organization are focusing on.

SHIFT

Perception plays a role as well. Do employees see themselves as being valued? How are people valued? For example, specific timelines are set in the high-tech industry to get their product out the door and to market before the competition does the same. I ask my clients, "What's important here? Is it the next release that counts? Are the small steps that happen every day noticed?" What is your company valuing? Do they acknowledge the human factor that makes the release happen? How do they celebrate individual contributions?

Celebration and the language used to celebrate success are critical ingredients in building more successes. If you are responding to concerns about moving forward with comments such as "try harder," you put your project at risk. You deplete the energy of your people by missing their contribution with this statement. What you focus on is exactly what you get.

What is valued in your professional life? Is it a bonus, a company car, a raise or a promotion that you reach for? The process is similar. When you set a goal and focus on reaching that goal it begins to come to realization. Tiny changes begin to take place in you. You begin to notice everyday occurrences in a different way. They may be so imperceptible that you only notice them when a colleague points them out. For example, the relationship with your boss begins to change. Maybe he offers a simple nod rather than the usual scowl. A peer calls to say she liked the way you handled a meeting earlier in the week. You notice each situation as "something different from the norm." The fact that you notice is an indicator of a new mindset. Perception is shifting. **When your mind shifts, new opportunities begin to appear.**

Until now I have been talking about the culture of work and how people perceive themselves as valued or not. Let's take a closer look at what's important in your personal life. Are the larger items such as a new car, a house, a promotion, recognition, better health, less stress or even a new relationship the ones that count? This is a significant question, the answer to which will help you see what's important in your life. When you think about your goal it starts to happen. Increments of change, ever so small, begin to appear.

A personal example comes to mind—where I noticed a shift in perception. Five years ago I was in the midst of a painful divorce. When I thought about my husband at that time, I wanted to make him wrong. I had totally forgotten that at one time we were very much in love. In fact, he was still a very good man. My friend Cindy reminded me, "There is a gift in everything, Janice. Your job is to find it. The more gifts you find in your current situation with David, the better your life will be."

SHIFT

Cindy was wise. David was not my problem, although he sure seemed to be at the time. My perception was my problem. There were old wounds to heal and healing the perceptions from childhood wounds takes time. We all have childhood wounds. I considered the gifts that he brought to my life over a 10-year period. Surprisingly enough, I began to feel better about my life.

There are gifts in absolutely everything that happens. If you are the leader, can you see these gifts? (See Chapter 11, "There is a gift in everything," for more on this.) They are often easier to see when looking back. The more you notice the gifts in your life, the more your working world improves.

In the early part of the book I mentioned that we change how we feel about the circumstances of our lives when we change how we think about these circumstances. The results are awesome. We slow down and live longer. Creative answers appear that address long-standing problems. We start to look after ourselves as if we were really important—and we are. We walk in the park, laugh and smell the roses. We appreciate moments in time. Stress levels drop. We acknowledge our own strengths. We appreciate our family, friends and colleagues more. And these are only a few examples. Noticing tiny changes on a daily basis is infinitely more important than waiting for those big changes.

André comes to mind. As we approached the end of our leadership development program, André noticed some changes in himself. "When I started this leadership program I noticed that all my decisions were black or white . . . no shades of gray." André learned in a period of a few months to let go of pushing others and to focus on changing himself. His effort to control his team made them less productive and increased everyone's stress, including his own. For example, if a report wasn't on his desk when he thought it should be, he tracked it down. Then he lectured about how "there are no acceptable mistakes." Needless to say, he found a rebuttal on every issue. He was rarely at peace, always dealing with the next verbal battle.

André's style has changed. Small steps have taken on a huge significance for him. Now he first notices his own irritation and makes a conscious decision to let the irritation go. He imagines that everything will happen in good order and at the exact right time regardless of where the team is at. Today André is rarely stressed. As he says, "Things just work for me. All that pressure was driving me crazy. It sure wasn't helpful for my team. And by the way, guess who created my stress?" André has let go of worry, anxiety and aggression. He is happier. His workday is highly productive. Trust is high on his team. The team is highly productive and efficient. A number of his team members have approached André to say they are more productive because of how he has changed. Something shifted in André's thinking. He is more in control now than when he was working to control others. A major shift happened when he let go of control.

EXERCISES

Has anyone called you lately to talk about a job opportunity for you in their company? Are you tired of the job you do? If so, recall an earlier conversation with a colleague about opportunities in other companies. How can you now fit into their hiring needs? What journals did you pick up recently that had information about that job you were looking for?

What tiny clues are you presented with on a daily basis that could help you achieve your goal? Search your mind for clues! What insightful gifts have you been given in the past hour?

Pay attention to new information, to non-material gifts and to concrete items that seem to come into your awareness over the next few days. Change is always happening. Are you always noticing?

21

Celebrate and celebrate.

The closing story belongs to Chris. It's about celebration and leadership techniques in uncharted waters, especially in his particular industry. Just to set the context—Sylvia, my business partner, and I have been working with his team for 15 months in our leadership development program. The entire purpose of this program is to have participants, many of whom are technical specialists, increase their skills in managing from the "people side" of change. They know their technical products very well and have had to balance their skills in managing their highly valued staff.

Over this 15-month period Chris's entire group, all participants in our leadership development program, accomplished major shifts in their leadership thinking and practices, changes they had not expected. Each month, either Sylvia or I met one-on-one with each of these senior executives. Our later meetings had focused on implementation of new leadership behaviors. We wanted to know how they were practicing

SHIFT

---

the new techniques and thought processes that they had learned. When we met with Chris the last day, he was grinning. Chris had a story to tell.

Two weeks earlier he had been given a new team to lead, all senior managers the next level down in the organization. Chris had set up a first whole-team meeting and the results had been spectacular. He was anxious to tell us about it. (For Chris's story in his own words see Appendix Three.)

Chris told us that he broke the ice by first having fun. He had his team members develop a personal motto, meet and greet each other and share their motto, and do things they had not done previously when teams had formed. For example, he had them find a teammate that was their exact height, another that shared the same birth month and still another who wore the same kind of shoes. They also talked about favorite drinks. Then he quizzed them on what they knew about their team members. "The purpose," he said, "was to release their demons, the limiting beliefs they had about work, their new leader and their colleagues."

He invited them to cross the chasm from the old ways of operating as a team to new ways where they would create new rules of how to work together. He talked with them about the transition model, the shift from traditional to collaborative thinking, the role of purpose and vision, and then he asked them to share ideas about themselves, their team and their organization. "My purpose is to teach, motivate and grow my people," said Chris. He asked them to notice how they resisted new ideas. The whole day was a celebration of coming together as a team and beginning to build a community of workers that focused on a shared goal.

Celebration is a way of slowing down. In order to celebrate you have to notice what is working. You have to feel good about what you're doing and decide on what you will be celebrating. Ask yourself, "How do I celebrate on a daily basis?" Notice the things you do well! Acknowledge yourself and your good work in various parts of your life.

The point I am making is this. There is always something else to do. With the pace of our lives today we are all racing to get things done, to complete work, to care for growing families, to organize sports lessons, dance lessons and ethnic language classes for our children and so on. No one else can slow your life for you. I work most often with engineers who want to spend time with their families and seem to find less and less time to do so. Dealing with life stress takes a concentrated effort to plan. With responsibilities piling up, there often seems to be no time to celebrate. Here is what I suggest:

SHIFT

At bedtime make a mental note of your accomplishments during the day. Share them with your mate or a good friend. Write them down. Notice where you are making a difference. Has anyone said thank you?

Call a colleague at work who works in another department and invite her to join you for a 10-minute walk outside. As you walk ask her what she is doing that she is proud of. Tell her of your accomplishments. Experience a sense of pride! Arrange to do this on a regular basis.

Invite a peer to have lunch with you in the cafeteria and exchange ideas about what is working on your team. Find out what works for them. Acknowledge the good work for each other.

Celebration isn't big. It happens in the moment. Often there is a bit of laughter and a shift in thinking. Celebrating accomplishments soothes our ego. Our self-esteem grows and we feel proud of ourselves. Our work improves. We smile and laugh more. People respond to us in positive ways. As one client put it, "Not only does my team celebrate major deliveries, I also insist that we celebrate mini-milestones, pebbles as we call them. This both helps the team jell and it ensures the team knows that management appreciates them."

EXERCISES

You give gifts to people you love. How often do you give to yourself? Feel this experience as if it had already happened. The feeling helps to make it happen.

Conclusion

The material you have covered in this book concerns the technology of human change. It is for you the individual leader and for the teams or team members who want to improve. While you know this is possible on a day-to-day basis you have found yourself repeating patterns that bring old results. The text has offered new ways of thinking so that you can leverage not only your new thinking, but also the dynamic ideas of others. Now that you have read various chapters and your own thoughts have been challenged you can shape what you want to do in your everyday work environment.

Remember the steps, the four principles of change. Start with yourself and note what is going on inside. Learn to identify this clearly and to tell the truth about what you feel and perceive. Then notice what works about your workplace and especially your part in it. Ask your boss, colleagues, team and especially yourself for what you want. These three steps seem easy. The last step is a bigger challenge. Start to notice that change is happening. The seeds of change are tiny and often imperceptible. Be still. Remember what you asked for and begin to notice that it is in fact happening. Your journey has begun.

Appendix One

Dr. Deming's 14 Principles of Quality Management

1. Adopt a new philosophy. Use the collective consciousness of all concerned.
2. Improve constantly and forever the system of production and service. Quality is management's responsibility.
3. Institute training at all levels in the organization.
4. Adopt and institute leadership. Focus on the vision and the outcome.
5. Drive out fear (discover its sources).
6. Break down barriers between staff areas.
7. Eliminate numerical quotas for the workforce; eliminate numerical goals for people in management.
8. Encourage education and self-improvement for all.
9. Take action to accomplish transformations.
10. Create constancy of purpose for improvement of production and service.
11. Cease dependency on mass inspection.

SHIFT

12. End the practice of awarding business on the basis of costs alone.
13. Remove barriers that rob people of pride of workmanship.
14. Eliminate slogans, exhortations and targets for the work.

Appendix Two

Testimonials About New Measures of Success

These comments come from a variety of leaders involved in our leadership development program in our client organizations. We consider them qualitative because they are the real perspective of our clients. They can't be measured quantitatively except by the client himself. For him or her they are real (internal) measures of success.

"I am able to look for the people aspect of change first rather than the components of a product. It helps me understand how my people are managing. When I do this first my people contribute to the other information that I need."

"Transition is now a clear process. I not only understand it but I can help my team through the various stages of transition (ending, neutral zone, new beginning). I am far more comfortable dealing with the unknowns because I know the answers will show up before long."

SHIFT

"People issues were killing us. Work just wasn't getting done. I thought pushing harder would make things happen when in fact the situation got worse. I learned to understand myself and in doing so began to understand others better. Now it's easy for me to get to the bottom of issues on a team. We then get on with the work that has to be done."

"The power of relationships has become a table stake. Nothing productive happens without relationships. At this point in my career my focus as a leader is almost always on improving relationships."

"I am generally more open and honest with my team and with my boss. I am far more able to ask directly for what I want and need. As a result, my team is much more able to complete the work that they are responsible for. My relationship with my boss is much healthier."

"Since much more of the unspoken is actually spoken on our team I am a better leader. I appreciate the risk-taking involved in good, clear, honest communication."

"Learning to appreciate the efforts of my team has been a plus. I am fanning the flames of recognition on a regular basis where I paid minimal attention to this before I joined our leadership development program."

"I have greater confidence, am more comfortable being myself and take greater risks in what I say and how I lead my team."

"When it comes to group dynamics, I now know what I am seeing and what to do to bring about change."

"My beliefs and values are clear to me. I am more comfortable to challenge my boss. Most of all I am able to let go of control so that the right results can happen."

"I am more aware of my own feelings. I feel more open and safe and have less fear to do the things that as a senior leader I must do. My team tells me that I am less competitive and more supportive and that they have become more cohesive as a team because of this."

"My team tells me that I have never been so in tune with them. They love it. They know that they can bring up anything and that I will do my best to help them work it through with them."

Appendix Three

Chris Applies New Leadership Skills

Chris, a team leader and an engineer, was introduced in Chapter 21. His courage and his ability to work differently as a leader had been strengthened and developed over the 15 months that he had spent in our leadership development program. Here is his story in his own words.

What a great day I had yesterday. I brought my new team together to build cohesiveness and to teach them what I have learned about leading. I want my team to work as a team so I decided to start right now. We met off-site to get away from the pressure of work. I told them to turn off their cellphones because we had some serious work to do to build our team. They were about to have fun. We did some unusual things to reduce their tension and to have some fun.

When new projects are started in a large development organization, one of the key challenges is building the new project team. The individuals selected to be on the team are usually a combination of people from recently completed projects, from recently cancelled projects, new hires and/or selectively from existing projects. The people are selected based on skill set, organizational structure and availability. They have no real sense of being a team.

Within large organizations, there is an underlying culture with numerous smaller cultures throughout. When creating new projects or organizations, these differences in cultures collide. These differences and the fact that members of the team have not worked together before are some of the key challenges that need to be overcome to make a project team effective. This effectiveness is established by getting to know one another, developing relationships and removing the barriers to communication.

I found myself in one of the above situations. I was just placed in charge of a software development team of 50 people consisting of new hires and two distinct cultures. To address the effectiveness issue, I created a session to remove some of the barriers. The main objectives of the session were to get to know one another and have some fun doing it. This was not your typical session. Most people in the organization are focused on doing their daily activities and do not understand

SHIFT

the importance of the human interaction required on large projects

I brought the group together in a large room and moved them outside their comfort zone. This was achieved by giving them a handout with pictures of everyone on the team and asking them to share with each other their personal motto. This was created with very little structure except for sorting them into common smaller groups. These sorts included favorite drink, area of birth, height and where they live. These smaller groups with some commonality (e.g., tea lovers) facilitated them opening up to each other to talk about interests, personal motto, etc. Some fun was introduced by identifying specific information on some of the members (e.g., who is the average height, who lives furthest from work). Other parts of the session focused on who is working on what, smaller groups to discuss ideas for change, and a fun quiz that required them to discuss the answers.

The feedback from the session was excellent. Comments included "what a great session," "well-thought-out session which really allowed us to meet each other and break the ice," "I forgot people at work can be like that and have fun," "great way to start a project," "I'm more enthusiastic about my work than I've been in ages."

All in all, team members had a great time, are inspired about the job, and have started to really get to know a lot of new colleagues and I expect over time new friends.

Appendix Four

Assess Your Profile as a Leader

The profile of a leader is counter-cultural and timely. Here is how he or she leads. On a scale of 1 to 10 (10 high) how do you rate your own leadership skills?

Vision: I see the whole picture and some of the major interventions long before others do. I design the plays and in the process I create and live with the vision.

1 2 3 4 5 6 7 8 9 10

Intuition: I experience inner tension and a sense of being on the edge much of the time. This is associated with my own understanding that I am different than the norm.

1 2 3 4 5 6 7 8 9 10

Trusts the timing of answers: I acknowledge that certain information cannot be available in advance. I trust that while answers are needed and not readily available, they are coming and will be available at exactly the right time. I don't worry about where the answers will come from. I just "know" they will come.

1 2 3 4 5 6 7 8 9 10

Synergy: I am able to link ideas about seemingly divergent activities, I know these ideas are part of a larger composite picture and a vision. During this process I use the power of silence and allow new thought to emerge, then I go into action. The organization responds positively and yet is often not sure about what I have done and what has actually happened.

1 2 3 4 5 6 7 8 9 10

Feelings: I am intimately in tune with my feelings. I know that my way to the solution is through the pain or difficulty of reaching the other side. I also know that feelings are the vehicle. My feelings act as an antenna to let me know if I am on track or not. I really trust my feelings and I know that many people don't.

1 2 3 4 5 6 7 8 9 10

SHIFT

Confidence: The counter-cultural aspect of my leadership style plays havoc with my confidence. I hesitate to ask for what I want and need and then I wonder if I am heard. I am learning that confidence is up and down. This is part of being human.

1 2 3 4 5 6 7 8 9 10

Spiritual: The power of my leadership style is internal, deeply connected to what Stephen Covey refers to as something greater. I strive for perfection, and seek to remember that I am already perfect in my learning in whatever stage I am in as a leader.

1 2 3 4 5 6 7 8 9 10

Balance: I believe in balancing work and personal life. Time for family and other special interests is sacred.

1 2 3 4 5 6 7 8 9 10

Leadership style: I take the visible stance of the leader when called to do so but much prefer to lead through influencing and supporting my team. I am described by my team as humanistic, authentic, credible, respected and experienced.

1 2 3 4 5 6 7 8 9 10

Service: I am one to serve others; I walk my talk and I have a great deal of integrity. What I say is what I do. I acknowledge my role when I have impacted others.

1 2 3 4 5 6 7 8 9 10

Bibliography

Abdullah, Sharif M. *The Power of One: Authentic Leadership in Turbulent Times*. Portland, OR: The Forum for Community Transformation, 1991.

Bennis, Warren. *Why Leaders Can't Lead: The Unconscious Conspiracy Continues*. San Francisco: Jossey-Bass Publishers Inc., 1989.

Block, Peter. *The Empowered Manager: Positive Political Skills at Work*. San Francisco: Jossey-Bass Inc., 1987.

Bolman, Lee G., and Terrence E. Deal. *Leading with Soul: An Uncommon Journey of Spirit*. San Francisco: Jossey-Bass Inc., 1995.

Bridges, William. *Transitions: Strategies for Coping with the Difficult, Painful, and Confusing Times in Your Life*. Boston, Mass.: Addison-Wesley, 1990.

Bridges, William. *Managing Transitions: Making the Most of Change*. New York: HarperCollins, 1990.

Bushe, Gervase R. "Being an Appreciative Self." In *The New Basics: Interpersonal Competence and Organizational Learning*. Vancouver: Simon Fraser University, 1999.

Champy, James. *Reengineering Management: The Mandate for New Leadership*. New York: HarperCollins, 1995.

Chopra, Deepak. *Ageless Body, Timeless Mind*. New York: Crown Publishers, 1994.

Covey, Stephen R. *The 7 Habits of Highly Effective People: Powerful Lessons in Personal Change*. New York: Simon & Shuster, Fireside, 1990.

Dannemiller, Tyson Associates. *Whole-Scale Change: Unleashing the Magic in Organizations*. San Francisco: Berrett-Koehler, 2000.

Davidson, Let. *Wisdom at Work: The Awakening of Consciousness in the Workplace*. New York: Larson Publication, 1998.

Deming, W. Edwards. *Out of the Crisis*. Cambridge, Mass.: Massachusetts Institute of Technology, 1986.

DePree, Max. *Leadership Jazz: The Art of Conducting Business Through Leadership, Followership, Teamwork, Touch and Voice*. New York: Dell Publishing, 1992.

DeSadeleer, Luke and Sherren, Joseph. *Vitamin C for a Healthy Workplace*. Carp, ON: Creative Bound, 2001.

Dyer, Wayne. *Wisdom of the Ages*. New York: HarperCollins, 1998.

Gershon, David, and Gail Straub. *Empowerment: The Art of Creating Your Life as You Want It*. New York: Bantam Doubleday Dell Publishing Group, 1989.

Hay, Louise. *The Power Is Within You*. Carlsbad, Cal.: Hay House, 1992.

Heider, John. *The Tao of Leadership*. New York: Bantam Dell Doubleday Publishing Group, 1988.

Hill, Napoleon. *Think and Grow Rich*. Scarborough, ON: Prentice-Hall, 1960.

Houston, Jean. *A Passion for the Possible: A Guide to Realizing Your True Potential*. New York: HarperCollins, 1997.

SHIFT

Jeffers, Susan. *Feel the Fear and Do It Anyway: Dynamic Techniques for Turning Fear, Indecision, and Anger into Power, Action, and Love*. New York: Ballantine Books, 1988.

Kabat-Zinn, Jon. *Wherever You Go There You Are, Mindfulness Meditation in Everyday Life*. New York: Hyperion, 1994.

LeBrun, Louise. *Fully Alive from 9 to 5: Creating Work Environments That Invite Health, Humor, Compassion and Truth*. Ottawa: Partners in Renewal Inc., 1999.

Pavelka, Joe. *It's Not About Time: Rediscovering Leisure in a Changing World*. Carp, ON: Creative Bound, 2000.

Quinn, Daniel. *Ishmael: An Adventure of the Mind and Spirit*. New York: Bantam Books, 1993.

Schaef, Anne Wilson. *The Addictive Organization*. New York: Harper & Row, 1988.

Von Oech, Roger. *A Whack on the Side of the Head: How You Can Be More Creative*. New York: Warner Books, 1990.

Weisbord, Marvin R. *Productive Workplaces: Organizing and Managing for Dignity, Meaning and Community*. San Francisco: Jossy-Bass Inc., 1987.

Wheatley, Margaret J. *Leadership and the New Science: Learning About Organization from an Orderly Universe*. San Francisco: Berrett-Koehler, 1994.

Janice Calnan is a specialist in the human side of organizational change. She brings a simple, powerful approach to innovation and leadership development. Janice brings her clients a blend of four professional careers and a deep understanding of how change works. Her track record demonstrates her ability to work with executives, managers and employees so that they can jointly design and implement appropriate change. For more information on Janice or her leadership development program, please visit her Web site at www.janicecalnan.com

Creative Bound Resources

a division of **Creative Bound Inc.**
Resources for personal growth and enhanced performance
www.creativebound.com

A speakers bureau with a unique offering! Our speakers are published experts in a variety of lifestyle areas, including stress control and life balance, motivation, leadership development and enhancement of personal and professional performance. They deliver their message in an upbeat, entertaining and accomplished fashion. Presentations are tailored to the needs and goals of each group for optimal impact.

Janice Calnan is a proven workshop facilitator and keynote speaker. She is available to speak on a variety of topics relating to *SHIFT: Secrets of Positive Change for Organizations and Their Leaders*.

To receive a complimentary information package,
including our **Guide to Products and Services,**
please contact Creative Bound Resources at 1-800-287-8610
or by e-mail at resources@creativebound.com

Some of our titles:

SHIFT: Secrets of Positive Change for Organizations and Their Leaders
Janice M. Calnan
0-921165-74-9
$18.95 CAN $15.95 US

Vitamin C for a Healthy Workplace
Luke De Sadeleer and Joseph Sherren
0-921165-73-0
$21.95 CAN $17.95 US

It's Not About Time: Rediscovering Leisure in a Changing World
Joe Pavelka
0-921165-69-2
$21.95 CAN $17.95 US

Resources for personal growth and enhanced performance
www.creativebound.com